G. SCREETON

20p

WHAT JESUS TAUGHT ABOUT . . .

BOOK 2

What Jesus Taught About . . .

Man, Sin, Repentance, Forgiveness, Salvation, Righteousness

HERBERT LOCKYER

VICTORY PRESS
EASTBOURNE

Published by arrangement with Harper and Row
Publishers, Inc., New York.

First British edition 1977

ISBN 0 85476 264 7

Printed in Great Britain for Kingsway
Publications Ltd., Lottbridge Drove,
Eastbourne, E. Sussex, BN23 6NT,
by Fletcher & Son Ltd, Norwich.

Contents

Introduction

Never since God endowed the first man with the power of speech has any human uttered more wonderful words than those leaving the holy lips of Jesus in the days of his flesh. His were not only "Thoughts that breathe, and words that burn," but mighty words that were to shape the destinies of men and nations. Down the ages multitudes have "wondered at the gracious words which proceeded out of his mouth" (Luke 4:22). The world at large agrees with the commendation of those Roman officers that "Never man spake like this man" (John 7:46). Wordsworth could liken those who had practiced the art of stately speech as having "Choice words, and measured phrases, above the reach of ordinary men."

But Jesus was never above the reach of ordinary man when he opened his mouth to teach. Many of "the common people who heard him gladly" were transformed through his "choice words, and measured phrases." What radiant garments his apt words were for his loving thoughts, even when spoken to the worst of sinners. They were always

> Wonderful words! Wonderful words!
> Wonderful words of life.

The lines of Cowper are truer of Jesus than of any other speaker:

> All his glorious language issued forth
> With God's deep stamp upon its current worth.

It was as a teacher that Jesus first began to gather disciples around him, and at the outset he established himself as the world's master preacher and teacher. Luke gives us a very lifelike portrait of Jesus when he stood up on a Sabbath morn in the synagogue at Nazareth to proclaim his first sermon. After reading from Isaiah's prophecy concerning his messianic mission (Isa. 61:1-2), Jesus commenced his teaching ministry by an exposition of the ancient prediction (Luke 4:16–30), and all eyes were fastened on him. That what he taught that morning blistered the consciences of some of his hearers is evident from the fact that they were filled with wrath and tried to silence the lips echoing forth such gracious words by killing the peerless teacher himself.

The Gospels present the ministry of Jesus under the three aspects of preaching, teaching, and healing. "Jesus went about all Galilee, *teaching* in their synagogues, and *preaching* the gospel of the kingdom, and *healing* all manner of sickness and all manner of disease among the people" (Matt. 4:23). The oral ministry is described by the terms *teaching* and *preaching*, there being twenty-four references to the former task, and fourteen to the latter, in the Gospels. Friend and foe alike gave Jesus the title of teacher, or rabbi, while the true insight of the four evangelists did not overlook the elements that made him a preacher who "was not without honor, save in his own country." That a distinction can be drawn between *teaching* and *preaching* is suggested by Dr. A. R. Bond in his *Study of the Homiletics of Jesus:*

> *Teaching* has for its purpose the instruction in principles and customs, whose acceptance may be reserved by the individual for his own convenience and deliberation.
>
> *Preaching* has to do with the public announcement of truth, with the intention to secure immediate response from the hearer. Both terms are used in the Gospels to record the same event, and distinctions in method and ideals are not being constantly observed, Luke 20:1. The Gospel of Mark is most faithful to the shades of meaning here. The preaching of Jesus in methods and purpose is described by two Greek words which mean—
>
> *The proclamation of a herald* and
> *The publication of good tidings.*
>
> While teaching and preaching would naturally contain common traits, *preaching* is a more comprehensive term, while the teachings of Jesus upon great themes belong to the departments of Theology and Pedagogy.

Although the preaching and teaching days of Jesus were few, through his manner and method and personal mastery of audiences, he not only created the Christian pulpit but influenced the homiletical presentation of truth down the ages. The history of oratory discovers the literary contribution to the preaching of Jesus. The pulpit is the distinctive produce of Christianity, and is ever effective when it combines a preaching and teaching ministry.

Before coming to an exposition of the varied themes or topics Jesus taught, attention must be drawn to the twofold way in which he appears as a teacher.

First, *he is prominent as an evangelical teacher.* Early in the teaching of Jesus was the invitation to repent and believe his gospel, seeing that the promises of the kingdom he came to proclaim were for those saved by his grace and power. Thus he labored to bring those who had ears to hear, a new way of life. In his encounter with Zacchaeus, Jesus declared that his mission in the world was to seek and save the lost (Luke 19:10), a mission of salvation Paul elaborated on when he declared that "Christ Jesus came into the world to save sinners; of whom I am chief" (1 Tim. 1:15). Such a redemptive task underlies many of the parables and sayings of Jesus, as, for instance, what he taught about the lost sheep, the lost silverpiece, and the lost son in Luke 15. Often he spoke of eternal life for those who repented of their sins and accepted him into their hearts (John 3:16). He distinctly says that he came to "call sinners to repentance" and that at Calvary he would give his life as a ransom for a lost world. Before his birth, he received the name *Jesus,* meaning "Jehovah is

Savior," since he was coming into the world as the Savior (Matt. 1:21). Thus we have John's affirmation: "In this was manifested the love of God toward us, because that God sent his only begotten Son into the world, that we might live through him" (1 John 4:9).

Many of the truths Jesus uttered were designed to emancipate the sin-bound from their shackles, as in the case of Zacchaeus. Think of the way in which multitudes of those who were weary and heavy laden found rest through his invitation to come to him (Matt. 11:28–30)! In this far-off day there are also myriads who can sing out of their redeemed hearts,

> I came to Jesus as I was,
>   Weary and worn and sad.
> I found in Him a resting place,
>   And He has made me glad.

Second, *Jesus is presented as an ethical teacher.* As an *evangelical teacher* Jesus taught those who were dead in sin where and how they could find eternal life, but as the *ethical teacher* he instructed those alive, in and through him, *how to live.* The saved must be sanctified and led to serve their Savior; the forgiven must learn how to be faithful. This brings us to the claims of Jesus in the very large realm of Christian and social ethics. While he did not develop any comprehensive system of social ethics, nor indeed of any kind of ethics, he did give specific precepts on many aspects of our life among men. In order to understand the full import of this ethical side of his teaching, it is necessary to understand what the world was like when Jesus came into it.

The character of his age was hard, lustful, cruel, idolatrous, and evil, making the virtues of men most difficult to maintain. Some idea of the corrupt conditions prevailing at that time can be gathered from Paul's revelation in Romans 1–3. Against such a background must we place the teachings of Jesus concerning righteousness, holiness, and social justice. The term *ethical* relates to moral action, motive, or character and also treats of morals, morality, or ethics. Many of our Lord's parables and proverbs are related to the way men should live and act in the varied relationships of life. Being concerned with human character and conduct, ethics, then, is not so much a subject of knowledge, but a source of action. They are associated with life or personality in its inward dispositions, outward manifestations, and social relations.

Chief among the teachings of Jesus on morality is the Sermon on the Mount, deemed by some writers to be impracticable in our kind of world. But as Dr. W. P. Patterson reminds us, "Though the Christian ideal towers high above the general practice of our generation, it may be that that practice will one day be looked back on as belonging to the half-savage practice of the world's youth. And in the present it has often been made sublimely practicable for those whom the Holy Spirit touched, and whose hearts were set aflame with a Christ-like love of man."

With our Lord's pronouncements of his ethics,

there was the promise of fulfillment. What he commands, he supplies. "Faithful is he that calleth you, who also *will do it*" (1 Thess. 5:24). His preaching of the kingdom may appear to be revolutionary, and because it meant to inaugurate a new society, it was so. It was so thorough in its whole conception that, for those who were satisfied with existing societies, it seemed to turn human relationships upside down and to be quite impracticable. But Jesus came into the world for no other purpose than to bring into existence a society consisting of those who by courage and faith should find his ethics practicable and make them real.

For a masterly treatment of every aspect of the ethical teaching of Jesus the reader is referred to the exhaustive articles by Drs. Archibald Alexander and James Stalker in *The International Standard Bible Encyclopedia.* Dr. Stalker has also a separate volume on *The Ethic of Jesus.* The subject of the Christian ideal, virtues, duties, and spheres of Christian activity based upon the moral teachings of Jesus is too vast a theme to be discussed here. Bishop Gore remarks that this "ethical teaching of Jesus was not expounded as a philosopher or legislator might expound a system. It was given by way of proverbs or aphorisms, sometimes highly paradoxical aphorisms—and parables." The purpose of the following pages is to prove this contention.

Approaching a classification of the teachings of Jesus, it is somewhat surprising how many topics he actually dealt with, and likewise their variety.

Further, no matter what theme he dealt with, he spoke "the truth, the whole truth, and nothing but the truth." Even his foes had to confess, "Master, we know that thou sayest and teachest rightly, neither acceptest thou the person of any, but teachest the way of God truly" (Luke 20:21). The answer Jesus gave to the question about taxes required by Caesar had great effect, for the questioners marveled at his answer and thereafter held their peace (Luke 20:26). The range of his teaching was remarkable and of such absorbing interest that it was no wonder that the people crowded in upon him and hung upon his words (Luke 19:3, 48).

The exact number of themes, topics, and subjects Jesus dealt with is not easy to decide since many of them are interwoven. Dr. W. Graham Scroggie in his *Guide to the Gospels* details forty of them. He observes that "we do not know the Gospels well enough until we have to some extent understood what Christ taught about these subjects, the study of which makes for our intellectual and spiritual enrichment." While it is popularly thought the teaching of Jesus implies what he said and taught as recorded in the four Gospels—and we are keeping, more or less, to what they reveal—elements of his teaching can be found in Acts and in the Epistles, and particularly in the Book of Revelation. Jesus gave the revelation of himself to John. That book contains seven letters of his which he sent to seven churches and which contain many precious gems of truth.

My controlling desire in the preparation of

these volumes is to present the teaching of Jesus in a way to attract you to the master teacher himself, who will ever remain without peer or rival in the history of oratory, profane or sacred. The Christless, sordid age in which we live requires a reemphasis of the saving and ethical truths the master taught, and it is my fervent prayer and hope that this presentation will assist many in witnessing about Christ and telling of his great teachings.

—1—

His Authority

In this designation of Jesus the term *authority* implies an independent commission from God that carried with it the power of its execution. It was somewhat fitting that Matthew should conclude his full report of our Lord's teaching, as enshrined in the Sermon on the Mount, with the observation, "He taught them as one having authority, and not as the scribes" (Matt. 7:29). This prolonged teaching period had a profound effect upon the auditors, for we read that when Jesus had ended his remarkable discourse "the people were astonished at his doctrine" (Matt. 7:28). The word for astonished implies *amazement* and suggests how overwhelmed the people were, not only by his teaching, but still more by himself, as he revealed the truth.

Two features impressed the rapt listeners, namely, the difference between Jesus and all other teachers ("not as the scribes"), and the authority he manifested ("he taught them as one having authority"). He spoke as if he were accustomed to receiving obedience from all. "Where the word of a king is, there is power" (Eccles. 8:4). Jesus never troubled himself about quoting authorities as the scribes were in the habit of doing. His was a God-given authority, born of infallible insight into the mind of God. Jesus never taught on personal authority as did the scribes in their dogmatic utterances. "My doctrine is not mine." His was the authority of God-inspired truth, not of personality.

The second observation of the people was that Jesus taught *not as the scribes.* We can only appreciate this remark if we know how and what the scribes taught. Alexander Whyte, in his rare work, *The Walk, Conversation, and Character of Jesus Christ Our Lord,* refers to the depths of imbecility found in the teaching of the scribes.

> Their own books, preserved to this day, prove to us that the New Testament, plain-spoken as it is, has not told us the half of the scandal of the life and teaching of the scribes and the Pharisees. You would simply not believe the frivolities, and the superstitions, and the downright immoralities of the teaching and preaching of the Scribes and the Pharisees, as all these things stand written in their own records. And it was the grace and the truth, it was the wisdom and the beauty of our Lord's teaching and preaching, all taken together with the heavenly holiness of life that led Matthew to give us such a full report of the Sermon on the Mount, and then to add to it this conclusion that our Lord did not teach as the Scribes.

The scribes were mere retailers of what others said. They loved to cite some great name to prove that their teachings were not original but approved by those with a renowned reputation for learning. Even today, writers and teachers are careful about quoting authorities and give authority for a statement for the advanced interpretation of Christianity, all of which has its value and makes for accuracy. But with Jesus it was totally different, as the people noticed. While he was always quoting Scripture, and taught how he was fulfilling it, he is never found quoting the rabbis of his time. This method was new to the scribes, who knew nothing of teaching what they had come to know from a heart-experience of intimacy with God, the source of truth.

These Jewish leaders were simply parrots, constantly repeating the learned traditions of their fathers—a method for which Jesus rebuked them. They knew nothing of the utterance of fresh, vibrant messages for the needy hearts they professed to teach. As for Jesus, his teachings were striking, apt, forceful, and of far-reaching influence. They also testified to his divine authority and of his sinless separateness from other teachers with whom he is often grouped and compared. Comparative teachers there may be, but the teacher sent from God is not one of them. Shakespeare reminds me that "Comparisons are odorous," and the matching of Jesus with ancient philosophers is one of these odorous comparisons, simply because none can be compared with him who is incomparable, separate, and supreme in the realm of pedagogy. "Who teacheth like him" (Job 36:22)?

There is no other explanation why the ethics he orally communicated in the small provinces of Galilee and Nazareth became the ethics of the world to live by. The teachings of Jesus have shaped the thinking of the world and are still shaping it. The man of Galilee was no dreamer, no mere visionary. The Gospels present him as an ardent revolutionary willing to suffer for what he taught. As T. R. Glover in his *Jesus of History* asks,

> When we make our picture of him, does it suggest the Man who has stirred mankind to its depths, set the world on fire, Luke 12:49, and played an infinitely larger part in all the affairs of men than any man we know of in history?

All who listened to Jesus in his itineraries, as well as multitudes all down the centuries who have studied his spoken word, testify that his speech was without parallel. There is never any real danger of overestimating his greatness. The risk is that of underestimating this most wonderful teacher the world has ever known, who transcends our categories and classification. We never exhaust him; and one element of Christian happiness is that there is always more in him than we supposed.

THE METHODS HE EMPLOYED

We now come to examine how Jesus put his authoritative message across. We know that he never had the countless volumes on homiletics that preachers and teachers have access to today to help him shape his public discourses. Because of his omniscience and omnipotence, he had no need to sit down and write and rewrite his messages, then tape them in order to mark their effect, and memorize them. In every opportunity that arose for public or private tuition, he knew exactly what to say and how to declare the truth required. Discussing the habits of Christ's mind, the way it moved and the characteristics of his thinking, Richard Glover wrote in *History of Jesus:*

> We note a certain swiftness, a quick realization of a situation, a character, or the meaning of a word. Men try to trap him with a question, and he instantly "recognizes their treachery," Luke 20:23. When they ask for a sign, he is quick to see what they have in mind, Mark 8:11–13. He catches the word whispered to Jairus—half hears, half divines it, in an instant, Mark 5:36. He is surprised at the slowness of mind in other men, Matt. 15:16; Mark 8:21. And in other things he is as quick—he sees "the kingdoms of the world in a moment of time," Luke 4:5; he beholds "Satan fallen like lightning from heaven," Luke 10:18–two very striking passages, which illuminate his mind for us in a very important phase of it. We ought to have been able to guess without them that he saw things instantly and in a flash—that they stood out for him in outline and colour and movement there and then.

Further, one cannot examine the teachings of Jesus without being impressed with his close observation of nature and of human life and relationship and with his economy of words in using these observations as illustrations of truth. He was never verbose. His language was always well chosen, simple, direct, and natural. It was likewise free from quotations, except scriptural ones. Then what a gift he had of arresting attention: "Whosoever will save his life shall lose it" (Matt. 16:25), which came with a spontaneous flash and lives in the memory. A notable feature of the sayings of Jesus is that they are hard to forget.

It is also evident that, along with other teachers of his time, Jesus did not teach, as we do in this highly developed age, by orderly, logically matured propositions. Ancient teaching was informal. There were no three-deckers—"firstlies," "secondlies," "thirdlies"—so common in Alexander Maclaren's *Expositions of Scripture*. However, Alexander Whyte tells us that Jesus always practiced an ancient rule of Greek and Roman oratory, though he had never learned the rules of any oratorical school:

> Out of the native wisdom of his own mind, and out of pure love of his heart, our Lord always "captivated the ears of his audiences" at the opening of all his discourses. What could be more conciliating, and indeed captivating, than the opening words of his very first sermon? What could take hold of a congregation better than the beautiful beatitudes with which he began his great Sermon on the Mount?

Some early centers of learning were known as *Peripatetic* schools because in them master and students walked about as they talked—which Jesus was fond of doing. Then before his time there was the famed *Socratic* method of informal question and answer, a method so common of our Lord's teaching. Even at the early age of twelve, Jesus had the gift of putting and answering questions (Luke 2:42–47). In fact, the questions he asked and others asked of him, and the answers he gave, as recorded in the Gospels, afford a profitable aspect of study.

Although Jesus sometimes taught formally, as in the synagogue or on the mountain side, much of his teaching was what we might call *table talk,* as scenes of teaching prove. Often his environment suggested answers to questions or subjects to be dealt with. Passing through wheatfields, walking along the roadside, or sitting by a wayside well prompted truths he wanted people to hear. Because of his omniscience he knew the questions men would ask of him before they were uttered, and so he was ready with a perfect answer, thereby causing those who heard him to be "astonished at his understanding" (Luke 2:47). In ancient times, "the city was the education, and the market-place the school where most of the most-abiding lessons were learnt."

Said the old Greek poet Simonides, "The city teaches the man," and it does, more than we realize. As we know, Jesus grew up in an Oriental town, in the middle of its life—a town with poor houses, bad smells and worse stories, tragedies of widow and prodigal son, of unjust judge and grasping publican—yes, and comedies too—all of which colored his public utterances. Human relationships likewise added their quota to his unique teachings. The education of Jesus was not bookish even though he may have had access to the works of prominent teachers and philosophers. Some writers claim to have found traces of other books in his teachings.

While Jesus was thoroughly immersed in the Old Testament, primarily, he found his education in home and shop, in the desert, on the wayside, and in the marketplace. As a boy, he watched those around him and weighed their words more closely than they guessed; their words provided "grist" for his mill. We sometimes say of preachers that their sermons "smell of the lamp," which means they are very bookish. But the illustrations and parables Jesus used in his teachings were full of humaneness and thus easily understood by his hearers.

Jesus had the art of taking experiences common to himself and to his audiences alike and using them to enforce his truths. His love of home, of bird and beast, and of the wild, open countryside as a country-bred peasant boy came through when he entered his public ministry. The lines of Wordsworth are so true if applied to Jesus:

> The earth
> And common face of Nature speaks to Us
> Remarkable things.

Much of the teaching of Jesus reveals the environment of his years of preparation. He was intimately associated with Galilee which was the center of many industries of the home and where there were factories of pottery and fine linen and dye-works. The caravans of the world's commerce passed through along the great trade routes. Dr. George Adam Smith reminds us that "Judea was on the road to nowhere; Galilee is covered with roads to everywhere." Thus, the life and scenes the boy Jesus looked out on were full of action, with Roman legions and the litters and equipages of wealthy noblemen passing to and fro. Then among the birds, animals, and flowers of the country, the child Jesus found much to interest his developing mind.

When, at about the age of fifteen, he left the village school to follow the trade of the home, Jesus became a carpenter and builder. The Aramaic word for "carpenter" means more than a worker in wood; it is also used to indicate a worker in stone (Matt. 13:55; Mark 6:3). Does not this practical experience at the bench and of outside construction lie behind Jesus' sayings connected with his trade? For instance, we have his references to the making of plows and yokes (Matt. 11:29, 30), lampstands (Matt. 5:15, 16), building of houses (Matt. 7:24–27), and barns (Luke 12:16–31). It is possible, then, to reconstruct from the range of Christ's teachings a picture of the kind of house and environment in which he lived before beginning his brief ministry at the age of thirty. Consider the following summary of his illustrations:

1. *Indoors*
   Women grinding corn (Luke 17:35)
   Heating the oven (Matt. 6:30)
   Making the bread (Matt. 13:33)
   Sweeping the floors (Luke 15:8)

Mending the clothes (Mark 2:21)
The value of money (Luke 15:8, 9)
Children at meals (Matt. 7:9–10)
Children in bed (Luke 11:7)

2. *Outdoors*
Flowers (Matt. 6:28)
Chickens (Luke 13:34)
Sheep (Luke 15:4)
Ox in a pit (Luke 14:5)
Foxes (Luke 9:58)
Eagles (Luke 17:37)
Small seeds, big trees (Mark 4:31, 32)
Sowing and reaping, wheat and corn (Matt. 13:24; Mark 4:3)
The marketplace, buying sparrows (Matt. 10:29; Luke 12:6)
bargaining (Matt. 5:33–37)
measuring (Luke 6:38)
children at play (Luke 7:32)
The sea, the dragnet (Matt. 13:47, RV)
the fishermen (Mark 1:17)

Further, his teachings suggest a wider outlook. They were not only parochial but universal, as the following aspects prove:

A nobleman who would seek a kingdom from Rome, which Archelaus, a son of Herod the Great, did (Matt. 2:22; Luke 19:12)
An ancient king with his slaves and dependents, great and small (Matt. 18:23)
Stewards, bad and good (Luke 12:42)
An unjust judge (Luke 18:2)
A banker (Luke 19:23)
A householder hiring laborers (Matt. 20:1)
Trading, in pearls (Matt. 13:45)

in oil (Matt. 25:9)
in weapons (Luke 22:36)
in cattle (Luke 14:19)
in slaves (Matt. 18:25)
in land (Matt. 13:44; Luke 14:18)

Robbery, on the road (Luke 10:30)
in the house (Matt. 6:19)

Marriage, groomsmen and maidens in attendance (Matt. 22:2; 25:1; Mark 2:19)

The burden of debt (Matt. 18:28)

The result of youthful dissipation (Luke 15:12)

The misuse of wealth (Luke 12:16-21)

The art of hospitality (Luke 14:7)

Prudent and eager resourcefulness (Luke 16:3)

The scribes and Pharisees (Matt. 23:2), the Sadducees (Mark 12:18–27), the publicans (Luke 18:9), the Samaritans (Luke 9:52), Gentile foes (Matt. 10:28)

Does not such a coverage of the lessons Jesus garnered from these varied aspects of life greatly help a living knowledge of him in his boyhood, youth, and manhood, which is in every way to be desired, since it is one of the chief objects of Christian education?

The life of women, as portrayed in some of Jesus' parables and sayings, is what he saw in his own mother's home, for example, the woman who lost part of her precious house-money (Luke 15:8–10), two women grinding at the mill (Luke 17:35), the housewife washing her crockery, outside and in (Luke 11:39), the woman hiding leaven in the meal (Matt. 13:33), a mother mending torn clothes (Matt. 9:16), the mother's task to satisfy healthy appetites of children who did not confine themselves to bread, but wanted fish and eggs as well (Matt. 7:10; Luke 11:11–12).

As the creator and lover of nature, Jesus drew many of his similes and metaphors from the birds of the air, the fish of the sea, and the fruits and flowers around. His teachings ever live because of their illustrations taken from sheep, oxen, hens, sparrows, foxes, eagles, and camels, sowing and reaping. Because Jesus knew nature, being on closer terms of intimacy than any other, the four facts he noted in nature are its mystery, its regularity, its impartiality, and its peacefulness.

As Jesus attended the village school and played with his school-fellows, he learned how they could be sulky at times (Luke 7:32). Some of the games of the children come out in his illustrations:

> At weddings and at funerals,
> As if His life's vocation
> Were endless imitation.

As to personal traits associated with his teaching, Jesus made much use of his eyes; so we have several references to his *looking* (Mark 3:5; 8:33; 10:23). Love, grief, and anger are emotions given of his looks. Jesus had feelings and expressed them, even in indignant utterances (Matt. 23:14; Mark 11:17). Characteristics of his mind as a teacher were a certain swiftness, a quick realization of a situation, a character, or the meaning of a word. Sometimes the scribes and Pharisees would try to trap him with a saying or a question, and he would instantly recognize their trickery and amaze them by his foreknowledge and swift reply (Matt. 9:11–13; Luke 20:23). We read that the Pharisees provoked "him to speak of many things . . . seeking to catch something out of his mouth, that they might accuse him" (Luke 11:53, 54). The more he preached to the Pharisees, the more bitter their opposition grew, until at last, determined to silence him, the cry arose, "Away with him, crucify him!" But those precious lips of his never uttered a single word which they could catch to bring an accusation against him.

PARABLES AND PROVERBS

It must be clear, even to the most casual reader of the Gospels, that Jesus had a unique way of using the popular medium of parables and proverbs. Further, he did not create the parabolic form of teaching, seeing there are many parables in the Old Testament. He at least developed it with high originality, and gave it a deeper spiritual import. Parables have the quality of making truth clearer to those who see the point. To others, without spiritual insight, they are only stories (Mark 4:11–12; Luke 8:18). Says Bishop Gore, "The parables of Jesus, as they appear in the world's literature are masterpieces, and are easily rememberable—we may almost say unforgettable." (See the author's volume, *All the Parables of the Bible.)*

As for the incomparable proverbs of Jesus, with their method of *parallelisms,* what pregnant maxims they are. For instance, when Jesus said, "He that is not with me is against me," the proposition is intelligible, and we can appreciate the truth expressed. All of his proverbs, it will be found, are principles stated in extremes, without modification, often requiring to be balanced by their seeming contraries. Studying the form of our Lord's teaching, we have to get at the *principle* behind the proverb, at the same time not forgetting that the short-pointed paradoxical form of instruction is meant to stimulate us, and to warn us that the conduct required of us in such and such cases will be extreme and difficult conduct, as in the somewhat hard proverb, "If any man . . . take away thy coat, let him take thy cloak also" (Matt. 5:40).

Bishop Gore reminds us of another Jewish habit of speech Jesus emulated, the building up of sentences on the framework of *not-but,* two hundred examples of which have been counted in the Gospels alone. "Labour *not* for the meat which perisheth, *but* for that meat which endureth unto everlasting life" (John 6:27). Some of the sayings of Jesus containing *not* and *but* mean exactly what is said, namely, that the first alternative is literally excluded. But more often it is intended only to depreciate the first by comparison with the second, as in the above Proverb, where Jesus certainly did not mean to condemn what he approves—honest work for an honest living—but only intended to fix our attention on a more important kind of labor.

All aspects of the teachings of Jesus, notably his precepts of admonition and instruction and chains of discourses, should be closely studied by those who are called to preach and teach the Word. The best-known example of the *chain* method is the Sermon on the Mount (Matt. 5–7), which, according to some writers, when compared with the Sermon on the Plain (Luke 6:20–49), creates the impression that the Evangelists strung various sayings together into a single discourse, or that they found them strung together that way in tradition. But the preface to the Sermon on the Mount suggests that it was a complete sermon delivered without any break. "When he was set . . . he opened his mouth, and taught [his disciples]" (Matt. 5:2).

THE RESULTS HE ACHIEVED

In H. Twell's heart-moving hymn, "At Even Ere the Sun Was Set," there is the line, "No word from Him can fruitless fall." The prophecy of Isaiah can certainly be applied to the matchless and eternal words leaving the holy lips of Jesus when among men. "So shall my word be that goeth forth out of my mouth; it shall not return unto me void, but it shall accomplish that which I please, and it shall prosper in the thing whereto I sent it" (Isa. 55:11).

Because of the divine source and substance of the teachings of Jesus, they cannot fail in their mission. "The word which ye hear is not mine," he could say, "but the Father's which sent me" (John 14:24). This, then, is the secret of the abiding influence of his utterances, and eternity alone will reveal the marvelous results of all Jesus taught while here below (1 John 2:14). We have, of course, the immediate effect of his teachings and the continuing influence of "the grace poured into his lips" (Ps. 45:2).

—2—

About Man

Jesus had every right to discourse about *man* because by his condescension he became the only perfect man the world has ever known. *Behold the man!* (John 19:5). And well might we behold him, for there was never before his like as a man, and there never will be again. As co-sharer in the creation of man, Jesus knew that he had been fashioned in the divine likeness, for was he not included in the plural, "Let *us* make man in *our* image, after *our* likeness" (Gen. 1:26)? Jesus, then, without whom "was not any thing made that was made" (John 1:3), knew everything about the constitution and purpose of man whom he assisted in creating.

From the dateless past, the Son of God, by his incarnation, became the Son of man, a title denoting an essentially human being and which he used of himself some eighty times in the Gospels. It is the title by which he most frequently designated himself. In passing, however, let it be said that although he became the Son of man, he was not the Son of *a* man. He is the only Son the world has known who did not have a human father. He was conceived of the Holy Spirit (Matt. 1:20). The terms, *Son of man* and *Son of God,* then, form a pair and aptly describe the two sides of our Lord's person, namely, his deity and his humanity.

Coming in the fashion of a man (Phil. 2:8), never man spake like this man, and all through the Gospels the humanity of Jesus is most evident. By becoming "the man Christ Jesus," he entered into a personal experience of human emotions, human desires, and human frailties, and his temptations, travail, trials, and tears have forever endeared him to mankind. Man is irresistibly drawn to him as he remembers that he is the one touched with his infirmities. He became like man, sin excluded. Although rich in his prerogatives in past glory, he became poor when he took upon himself frail flesh to die as man's deliverer.

Being man, Jesus knew what was in man and was able to penetrate his thoughts and read his intentions. He could teach more clearly than the philosophers of his time about the vital problems of man's destiny because he had known it from the beginning of mankind. When Jesus entered his public ministry of preaching and teaching, man was asking:

> But what am I?
> An infant crying in the night;
> An infant crying for the light;
> And with no language but a cry!

Jesus understood such yearnings and answered this infant cry with himself. As Dr. A. R. Bond movingly puts it in his most remarkable volume, *The Master Preacher:*

> Upon his heart fell the shadows that saddened others; the minor chords of human woe made his own heart-strings quiver with the sympathetic melody; the threnody of misfortune and the dirge of death found a response in his tenderness and help. He entered into fellowship of a common life with his fellow-men, alive to their disappointments, touched by the feeling of their infirmities, tempted with their struggles, and able to succour every tempted soul. He knew the trials, aspirations, and needs of men, for his insight into life was piercing, comprehensive, clear, and interpreted by his own experience.
>
> His words were authoritative with the strength of a fulness of his entrance into the entire life of the world. His mind and heart garnered the full harvest of human experience, excluding the thorns and thistles, which they could not house. His preaching caught the authority of the double relationship. Out of his complete Divine Sonship he could bring the message which could be applied according to his knowledge of men that he brought from his complete human Sonship.

These, then, are the thoughts to have in mind as we consider what Jesus had to say concerning man. By reason of his birth when, as God, he became flesh, he had a complete experience of human nature and complete knowledge of man (John 2:24–25; 4:29).

> Touched with a sympathy within, He knows our feeble frame:
> He knows what sorest trials mean for He has felt the same:
> But patient, undefiled, and pure the great Redeemer stood,
> While Satan's fiery darts He bore, and did resist to blood.

Since no man knows the things of a man like the man of Galilee, let us now try to piece together what he taught about man whom Lord Byron described in "Manfred" as "Half dust, half deity, alike unfit/To sink or soar." I prefer St. Augustine's appraisal: "Man wonders o'er the restless earth, the flowing waters, the sight of stars, and forgets that of all wonders, man himself is the most wonderful."

MAN IS A DUAL BEING

Jesus taught that man has a spiritual side to his make-up as well as a physical, that he is soul and spirit as well as body. Is this not borne out in his reply to Satan during the temptation in the wilderness? Throughout this severe testing period lasting forty days and forty nights, Jesus fasted and at the end of the satanic onslaught was very hungry. "He had not felt the need of food while absorbed with the contemplation of the work on which he had now entered," says Richard Glover in *History of Jesus*. "But when the strain is over, he found himself helpless and feeble through want of bodily sustenance" (Matt. 4:1–3; see Mark 3:20, 21; John 4:31, 32).

Tempting Jesus to assuage his hunger by displaying his omnipotence, tauntingly Satan said, "If thou be the Son of God, command that these stones be made bread." Then came the crushing reply of Jesus based upon Deuteronomy 8:3: "Man shall not live by bread *alone,* but by every word that proceedeth out of the mouth of God" (Matt. 4:3, 4). Jesus needed bread, for he was hungry; and man must have the bread he is able to bake for his physical needs which Jesus himself recognized when he taught men to pray, "Give us this day our daily bread." But the question arises, If, in the first miracle he performed, Jesus turned the water into wine to meet a need at the marriage feast in Cana, why did he not respond to the seemingly harmless suggestion to provide the bread he certainly required being "an hungered"? One imperative lesson we must learn in life is that every act is wrong which is done from wrong motives, however innocent in itself it may seem to be. Had Jesus displayed his power and made the bread he required, he would have yielded to the doubt Satan insinuates in his question.

Jesus went on to give us one of those arrestive *buts* of his: "But by every word that proceedeth out of the mouth of God." Material bread is necessary to sustain life in the body; Jesus, the Word of God, is the bread of heaven to nourish the spiritual side of man (John 6:26–35). The folly of man today is to live for bread alone. He obeys the tempter's voice, *Make bread!* Thus he lives only for the gratification of the physical side of his being, forgetting that he is also a "living soul" (Gen. 2:7), for whom food has been provided both in the written and in the living Word.

All around us are multitudes very much alive physically but dead spiritually. Speaking of widows, Timothy writes, "She that liveth in pleasure is dead while she liveth" (1 Tim. 5:6). There were church members in Sardis of whom John wrote, "Thou hast a name that thou livest, and art dead" (Rev. 3:1). Such may appear to be paradoxical, but far too many are alive yet dead. They make every provision for their material and natural needs but are not mindful of the deeper need of the soul for the true bread from heaven. Would that we could hear those who live only for bread for the body cry, "Lord, evermore give us this heavenly bread of life the soul must have!"

MAN HAS AN INHERITED EVIL NATURE

Jesus did not believe that in every man is the divine spark, nor did he teach that "God is slumbering in the heart of every man, and only needs to be awakened." Running through all his references to the heart of man is the Old Testament truth that man was born in sin or born with an evil nature with propensities toward iniquity. He knew, as no other, that in unregenerated man there was no good thing, that his throat was an open sepulchre, with the poison of asps under his lips (Rom. 3:9–20). Think of our Lord's scathing exposure of the professedly religious Pharisees: "O generation of vipers, how can ye, being evil, speak good things? . . . An evil man out of the evil treasure bringeth forth evil things" (Matt. 12:34, 35). "If ye then, being evil [not only *doing* but *being* evil]" (Luke 11:13). "Out of the *heart* of man proceed evil thoughts . . . All these evil things come from within, and defile the man" (Mark 7:20–23).

He who was without sin knew perfectly well the evil of which the human heart is capable (Matt. 15:19) and all about falsity, even in professed religionists (Matt. 15:8). When Paul spoke of "the natural man," he meant man as he is *naturally* sinful and used this figure of speech for that evil nature common to all men and which is equivalent to our Lord's phrase about men "being evil." Descriptions like "sinful inclination," "evil disposition," "apostate will," "original sin," and "native depravity," which theologians use, all imply the same truth Jesus taught, namely, that man is born with a bias toward evil and needs to be reborn by the Holy Spirit and made a new creature in Christ Jesus, or "the spiritual man." Proud, obstinate man may reject what Jesus taught about his heart corruption and lost estate, but in his vain effort to reform himself he knows only too well that there is an evil force in his nature beyond his control which can only be dislodged by a greater power than himself.

MAN IS CAPABLE OF GREAT WICKEDNESS

Because of the poisoned well within man, in no uncertain terms Jesus described the putrid waters capable of flowing from a tainted source. "Out of the abundance [the overflow] of the heart the mouth speaketh" (Matt. 12:34). This is true of purity as well as impurity. Everything depends on what a man *wills*. Says Richard Glover in *Jesus and Man:*

> It is the inner energy that makes a man; what he says and does is an overflow from what is within—an overflow, it is true, with a reaction. It is what a man *chooses,* and what he *wills,* that Jesus always emphasizes:
> *God knoweth your hearts* (Luke 16:15).

Jesus used the illustration about the impossibility of a good tree bearing corrupt fruit or a corrupt tree producing good fruit (Matt. 7:15–20). Then, in his teaching regarding the defiling streams coming out of a man, Jesus listed the manifestations of wickedness to expect:

"Evil thoughts, adulteries, fornications, murders, thefts, covetousness, wickedness, deceit, lasciviousness, an evil eye, blasphemy, pride, foolishness" (Mark 7:21, 22).

Knowing all there is to know about man, is it not amazing that in spite of all the sin he is capable of, Jesus was mindful of him and gave his precious blood to make even the vilest clean?

MAN IS A LOST SINNER

In his teaching concerning man, Jesus often used the word *lost,* and no other descriptive term is as fitting as this, for man is a lost being. Through the Fall, he lost the original powers with which his creator endued him. Robert South, in a famous sermon, said that "Aristotle was but a wreck of an Adam, and Athens but the rubbish of an Eden." How completely sin has defaced the divine image in man! That man has lost his righteousness and happiness is clearly evident as we look at the state of the world today!

But masses of lost souls mattered to Jesus who summed up his work in the world as he met one of them in the squalid little figure of a man, Zacchaeus, whom people around despised. "The Son of man is come to seek and save that which was lost" (Luke 19:10). Zacchaeus was one of these, but Jesus came into his life, and the man held in contempt became a transformed person and a pioneer of Christian generosity (Luke 19:1–10). Then the taunt flung at Jesus really described what he was and wished to be: "The friend of publicans and sinners" (Luke 7:34; Mark 2:16).

The constant foes of Jesus, the scribes and the Pharisees, tried to fill the cravings of the lost for God with the Law; and when the Law failed to satisfy such a yearning, they had nothing further to suggest, except their fixed ideas. "God heareth not sinners" (John 9:31). But Jesus taught that his Father did care for and hear sinners. The religious leaders left the masses alone, having no feelings whatever about them being as sheep without a shepherd. Jesus taught that God loved them so much as to give him, his only-begotten Son, that they might be saved (John 3:16). Is not this truth illustrated in the threefold parable of the lost Sheep, the lost coin, and the lost son (Luke 15)?

> I was lost, but Jesus found me,
> Found the sheep that went astray.

The term *lost,* however, has a twofold implication, namely, something lost with every possibility of recovery or something lost with no possibility of recovery. Our railways have what they call the Lost Property Office. Goods, lost or left behind by passengers, are held so that they can be applied for and reclaimed. But when there is an air disaster and the report is printed of all who died, the usual phrase employed is, "All lives on the plane were lost." Alas! for them there was no recovery, save as charred corpses.

This twofold significance is attached to the word *lost* as Jesus used it. He came across many who were lost in sin, like the woman taken in adultery, but he found her, as the shepherd found the lost sheep. No matter how lost a soul may be, while the door of mercy stands ajar, he or she can be recovered by the seeking Shepherd. According to Paul's testimony, in him the Savior recovered the chief of sinners.

Jesus also taught the further implication of the word *lost,* namely, something lost with *no* possibility of recovery. If the lost determine to remain lost, despising the salvation offered them, then, dying in their sins, they die lost forevermore. "If ye believe not that I am he, ye shall die in your sins" (John 8:21, 24). When Jesus spoke of a man "losing his own soul," he implied an *eternal* loss as well as a present one. Then when he taught that if men finally reject him as their only Redeemer, they must certainly *perish,* such a term does not mean annihilation or cessation of being, since man is immortal, but everlasting banishment from the presence of a thrice holy God (John 3:16; Rev. 20:15; 21:27).

MAN'S SOUL IS OF INESTIMABLE VALUE

Shakespeare's Hamlet exalts God's masterpiece in creation in this fashion:

> What a piece of work is a man! how noble in reason! how infinite in faculties! in form and moving how express and admirable! in action how like an angel! in apprehension how like a god!

While sin has debased man's nobility and changed him from being angellike into a diabolical creature, in his purest form he is still a reflection of his creator. The incomparable value of man's soul makes understandable the mission of Christ as a Redeemer. Synesius, who lived about A.D. 410, wrote that "A thing of price is man because for him Christ died." In his estimation of man's worth, Jesus said that he is more valuable than the entire universe. "What is a man profited, if he shall gain the whole world, and lose his own soul? or what shall a man give in exchange for his soul" (Matt. 16:26)?

Because the vital loss of soul is irreparable, its redemption is most precious (Ps. 49:8), and nothing less than the precious blood of the sinless man can avail to restore him to what his Maker intended him to be. Through grace, man receives still higher value as a member of the body of Christ who assured his own that the very hairs of their head were numbered and that they were of more value than many sparrows. What a tragedy, then, for God's supreme handiwork to languish in hell!

To lose one's wealth is much,
To lose one's health is more,
To lose the soul, is such a loss
That nothing can restore.

MAN MUST REPENT AND BE REGENERATED

A sinner by birth, then a sinner by practice, man must repent of his sin and be born anew by the Spirit of God in order to become a "new man." The pathway from his sinnership to his saintship consists of three steps: (1) "Repent ye" (Mark 1:15; Luke 15:10); (2) "Come unto me" (Matt. 11:28); and (3) "Follow me" (Matt. 4:19).

Jesus came calling sinners to repentance, for if they remain ignorant of their condition, they will never realize the necessity of regeneration. To Nicodemus, a man deeply religious and highly educated, Jesus said, "Ye must be born anew" or "born from above." It is sadly possible for a man to be sincerely religious and yet not be a Christian after the standard of Christ. "Except a man [religious or irreligious] be born again, he *cannot* see the kingdom of God" (John 3:3–7). Man may think that his own righteousness is a sufficient passport into the kingdom, but all his righteousnesses are as filthy rags in God's sight. So whether he is good or bad, a man must come to see that he is a beggar on God's grace and mercy and that unless he comes to him in his way, and on his terms, he is a lost sinner in danger of eternal condemnation.

Jesus alone claims to be the Savior of man, the satisfier of his deepest needs and the giver of rest to his burdened soul (Matt. 11:28; John 7:37–38). He asks nothing of sinners but genuine sorrow for sin and unreserved surrender to his claims. But once a person becomes a Christian, Jesus demands all that he is and has, and that thereafter nobody and nothing must interpose between himself and the soul of his follower.

BIBLE STUDY QUESTIONS

Take time to turn to each Scripture reference and mark the verse or a portion in your Bible.

1. In what ways was Jesus uniquely different, yet one with all mankind?

2. How did Jesus show us that spiritual and physical gratification are both necessary?

3. Describe the condition and character of the lost sinner.

4. Explain what is required of man in each step from sinner to "new" man.

— 3 —

About Sin

Much of what we have said about the nature of man is also relevant under this section. Having seen something of the *fruit* of sin in him, we now consider the *root* of sin, or what Jesus taught about this intrusion into God's universe. The tragic fact of sin is involved in Christ's doctrine of man. It is taken for granted that we cannot formulate a complete doctrine about sin from the few scattered references to it by Jesus in the four Gospels. For this, we need the coverage of the Bible as a whole. Confining ourselves, therefore, to what the Master taught about this topic, we observe the following features (see my book, *All the Doctrines of the Bible*).

First, Jesus could not have ignored the problem of sin even if he had wished to ignore it, for he came into the world to die for its sin. Before his birth, he was called *Jesus,* a name implying that he would save people from their sin (Matt. 1:21; John 1:29). Sin was the keynote of the preaching of John the Baptist, who was likewise the herald of the sinless Lamb who would bear away such sin. Dr. Alexander Whyte points out:

> If we would enter truly into any of our Lord's texts, and would really and truly take home to ourselves any of our Lord's sermons, we must continually keep in mind what, exactly and exclusively, his errand was in the World. *SIN* was his errand in the World, and it was his only errand. He would never have been in this world at all, either preaching sermons, or doing anything else, but for *SIN*.
>
> He could have done everything else for us without coming down into this world at all; everything else but take away our sin. And thus it is that our sin is the key wherewith to open up all he ever did, and all he ever said, while he was with us in this world. And thus it is also that unless your sin is ever before you, neither Jesus Christ himself, nor his coming, nor any of his texts, nor any of his sermons, will ever be understood by you.
>
> You will not understand or comprehend one single clause of his first text, Luke 4:16–19, nor one single sentence of my present sermon upon his first text, unless you attend all the time as a sinner, and as nothing else but a sinner. You must be poor, as only a sinner is poor.

T. R. Glover's chapter, "Jesus' Teaching about Sin," in his *Jesus of History,* shows how our Lord's view of sin is very different from those current in that day.

> Man set sin down as an external thing that drifted on to one like a floating burr—or like paint, perhaps, —it could be picked off or burnt off. It was the eating of pork or hare—something technical or accidental;

or it was (many thought) the work of a demon without, who could be driven out to whence he came. Love and drunkenness illustrated the thing for them —a change of personality induced by an exterior force or object, as if the human spirit were a glass or a cup from which it could be emptied and the vessel itself remain unaffected.

Jesus has a deeper view of sin, a stronger psychology, than these, nor does he, like some quick thinkers of today, put sin down to a man's environment as if certain surroundings inevitably meant sin. Jesus is quite definite that sin is nothing accidental—it is involved in a man's own nature, in his choice it comes from the heart, and it speaks of a heart that is wrong.

JESUS SPOKE MUCH ABOUT SIN

"He that is without sin among you, let him first cast a stone" (John 8:7). Jesus was the only one who ever lived without sin; yet he never cast a stone against a sinful woman taken in adultery.

"Whosoever committeth sin is the servant of sin" (John 8:34; 9:24).

"If I had not come and spoken unto them, they had not had sin: but now they have no cloak for their sin" (John 15:22).

"He will reprove the world of sin" (John 16:8, 9).

"He that delivered me unto thee hath the greater sin" (John 19:11).

"Behold the Lamb of God, which taketh away the sin of the world" (John 1:29; 18:14).

JESUS CALLED MEN SINNERS, OR MEN LIVING IN SIN

"I am come to call . . . sinners to repentance" (Matt. 9:13).

"The Son of man is betrayed into the hands of sinners" (Matt. 26:45).

"Sinners also love those that love them" (Luke 6:32, 33).

"Sinners also lend to sinners to receive as much again" (Luke 6:34).

"God be merciful to me a sinner" (Luke 18:13; 19:7; John 9:24).

"A friend of . . . sinners" (Matt. 11:19).

"Suppose ye that these . . . were sinners above all men" (Luke 13:2, 4).

Chief among those Jesus named sinners were the publicans, Pharisees, and Sadducees. As Professor Stalker points out, they represented three notorious forms of *sin,* each of which lay like a burden on Jesus' spirit till he relieved himself in their exposure and condemnation.

The sin of the publican. Jesus linked "publicans and sinners" and "publicans and harlots" together, for these were the "lost sheep," those who had broken through the fences of religious and social observance by which Jewish life was regulated and distinguished from the world at large, thus allowing themselves to become a reproach and a menace to all by whom these barriers were respected. The Pharisees and scribes, observing how the publicans and sinners were eager to hear Jesus preach and teach, murmured among themselves, "This man receiveth sinners, and eateth with them" (Luke 15:2).

But who and what were these publicans, the most despised sinners among sinners? In Britain, *publicans* are those who run "public houses," or drinking saloons, in which intoxicating liquors are sold and drunk. But in our Lord's day publicans were tax gatherers or farmers. The Herods auctioned to the highest bidder the right to exact and collect taxes in specific areas. The buyer would subdivide the area and auction portions of it to smaller men. Agents employed in the actual collecting of the taxes were called *publicans.* Naturally these public tax gatherers wanted to retrieve as soon as possible the money they had "staked," with the result that in the main they were *extortioners* (Luke 3:12, 13; 19:8). The fact that degenerate Jews would serve the Romans and the Herods in this way made them hated and despised (Matt. 9:10–13), and they were looked upon as having forfeited their nationality and gone over to the pagans. Thus, the very worst that could be said of any man was that he was "an heathen man and a publican" (Matt. 18:17).

Yet the attitude of Jesus to this lowest type of sinner was one of the most singular and characteristic features of his ministry. Little of his indignation was directed against those guilty of carnal and public sins. His scathing denunciations were reserved for sinners of a wholly different cast. Toward the publicans Jesus manifested a surprising leniency, not to say partiality. His enemies were not lying, then, when they condemned him as "a gluttonous man, a friend of publicans and sinners." Jesus attended a feast that Matthew, originally Levi the publican, gave at his house. When Jesus went home with Zacchaeus, chief among the publicans, the Pharisees chided that he had gone to be a guest with a man who was a sinner (Luke 19:7; see Matt. 11:19; Luke 7:34).

But those publicans and sinners with whom Jesus was so friendly never received the impression that he was condoning their manner of life or that he was making himself one of them. They were perfectly aware that Jesus had come to save them from the evil way of life—which he did! He was not blind to their faults, but he never forgot that they were human beings worth restoring, hence, his astounding statement that "the publicans and harlots" would enter his kingdom before the carping priests and elders (Matt. 21:23, 31). Matthew became a disciple and was chosen as one of the twelve (Matt. 9:9; 10:3). Fitting, is it not, and somewhat dramatic, that unjust taxation—that historic root of bitterness through past ages—should end in contemplation of Jesus who said to an outcast and guilty tax collector, the words summarizing his mission on earth: "The Son of man is come to seek and to save that which was lost" (Luke 19:10).

The sin of the Pharisee. Originally, the Pharisees were a commendable party. Their group probably arose as a protest against the encroaching Greek influence, before the time of the Maccabees, which led them to adhere even more strictly than was necessary to the old Mosaic ways. During

Jesus' day there were a few Pharisees who remembered these worthy foundations. Saul of Tarsus who became Paul the apostle was not ashamed of having been one of this minority (Acts 23:6; 26:5–7). Gamaliel, also, was a good example of the better sort of Pharisee (Acts 5:34).

As a party, however, the Pharisees degenerated into an assembly of talkers rather than actors. Religious hypocrisy became their most glaring sin which called forth some of the most scathing denunciations to leave the tender lips of Jesus (Matt. 5:20; 16:6, 11, 12; 23:1–39). If it seemed as if he displayed extraordinary tolerance to the sins of the publicans and harlots, he made up for it by his blunt exposure of the Pharisees. What contempt he poured upon them in his Sermon on the Mount when he turned into ridicule their habits of prayer, fasting, and almsgiving! To him, they were sinners far worse than the publicans, whom the Pharisees hated, because their sins were of a religious nature. How Jesus scorned their holy-looking dress, long prayers, and lip-sermons! Of these professed religious teachers Jesus said, "They say and do not." He had no hesitation in calling them "children of the devil."

The most direct collision with these religious hypocrites is preserved for us in the sermon of Jesus to the multitudes and to his disciples, recorded for us in Matthew 23. In tones ranging from the most biting sarcasm to holy indignation Jesus exposed the Pharisees, his avowed enemies. He named them "children of hell" and compared them to "whited sepulchres, which indeed appear beautiful outward, but are within full of dead men's bones, and of all uncleanness." Then came his Seven Woes in which he revealed how the Pharisees had carried iniquity to the point of perfection. Their glaring sin was a foreshadowing of "the mystery of iniquity," and its wickedness was not realized by the populace because it masqueraded in the garb of sanctity. The poor publicans knew they had plenty to repent of, but the Pharisees were not aware of anything for which repentance was necessary. In fact, they seemed incapable of repentance.

Shakespeare, in "Love's Labour Lost," says, "Now step I forth to whip hypocrisy," which Jesus did most mercilessly, and how those Pharisees cringed under the whip! Laurence Stern, of the seventeenth century, wrote that "Of all the cants which are canted in this canting world, the cant of hypocrites may be the worst." Jesus thought it was and thus sought to destroy such a false, religious mask. In Matthew 23, Jesus denounces hypocrisy as so great a sin. In expository fashion Richard Glover elaborates on this helpful outline in *History of Jesus*:

Hypocrisy is a hard taskmaster (23:4).
Hypocrisy lives only for the praise of men (23:5–7).
Hypocrisy is most mischievous (23:13–22).
Hypocrisy concerns itself with the small things of religion (23:23, 24).
Hypocrisy deals chiefly with externals (23:25–28).
Hypocrisy reveres only what is dead (23:29–32).
Hypocrisy finds a fearful judgment (23:32–36).
Hypocrisy receives an unexpected lament (23:37–39).

While the vice of hypocrisy today may differ from the way the Pharisees condoned it, combining as they did "the maximum of formalism with the minimum of reality," and although we may have no intention of falsity, we may maintain habits and ways after the feelings which originated them have died away, leaving us as hypocrites. The sure and only cure for any tendency to such a sin is to live beneath the eye of God, with all its infinite comfort and constraint. Deceit is an abhorrent sin in his sight. As this is a vice specially besetting all who inherit a religious life and creed, which they are unwilling to let go, but have no devotion enough to keep up—a sin, therefore, easily besetting those who have Christian homes and Christian upbringing,—we should give heed to the Savior's lessons on it. Perhaps the most moving words Jesus ever uttered were those where he was found lamenting over those who would not let him show that, although he severely upbraided such sinners, he loved them in the midst of their wickedness and hypocrisy. "I would . . . ye would not."

The sin of the Sadducees. The Sadducees, further enemies of Jesus, were named after Zadok, or Sadduc (2 Sam. 8:2), the high priest, the most important founder of a branch of the priesthood, and a descendant of Aaron (1 Chron. 24:3). Between the Pharisees and Sadducees there were marked differences. The former were traditionalists, while the latter, a Jewish politico-religious party, took their guidance from Scripture alone and not from the ruling of the elders. The Sadducees denied the Pharasaic doctrine of the resurrection of the body and of existence in hell; they also rejected the reality of angels (Mark 12:18; Acts 23:8) and the rewards and punishments of a future life.

The Sadducees not only denied the immortality of the soul and the resurrection of the body, they also rejected the traditions of the Pharisees who believed that Moses delivered the doctrine of a future life to the elders (Acts 23:8). Josephus asserts that this party believed that the soul dies with the body and that there is no divine providence. In their encounter with Jesus in regard to the resurrection, there is an element of contempt implied in the illustration which they used as an indication they did not take him seriously (Matt. 22:25; Mark 12:20; Luke 20:29).

Nevertheless, the Sadducees were afraid of the effects of Jesus' teaching and united with the Pharisees to interfere with his mission and to destroy the church he came to build (Matt. 16:1–4; 22:23–33; Acts 4:1–22; 23:6–10). Although the doctrines and practices of the Sadducees were conspicuously alien to the teachings of Jesus and to the conduct he enjoined, he did not denounce them as he did the Pharisees. In fact, he never rebuked them save along with their opponents the Pharisees; whereas he frequently denounced the Pharisees alone. The Sadducees seemed to look upon Jesus as a harmless fanatic who, by his strong denunciations of the Pharisees, was weakening their influence much to the satisfaction of the Sadducees.

This aristocratic and somewhat priestly party

did not play anything like so important a part in the life of Jesus as did the Pharisees. He did not confront the Sadducees nearly as often as he did the Pharisees. Only at the very end of his ministry do we find the Sadducees openly identified with the opposition to the influence and teaching of Jesus. Only when he claimed to be the Messiah did they become more vocal and promptly decreed his arrest and death. The arrest of Jesus, however, was to be in secret, "lest a tumult arise among the people" (Matt. 26:5). Later on, Paul, although a Pharisee, was an agent of the Sadducean high priest in the persecution of the church. It is interesting to observe that after the resurrection the Pharisees became less hostile to the followers of Jesus; but the Sadducees maintained their attitude of suspicion and hatred (Acts 4:1).

While the Sadducees were not as numerous as their opponents the Pharisees, theirs was a prominent sect, and priestly descent had an influence comparable to their rivals. They were a political party, of priestly and aristocratic tendency, as against the more religious and democratic Pharisees. They were a skeptical party whose religious beliefs lacked warmth and conviction. They gained, however, complete ascendancy in the Sanhedrin, and later, under the leadership of Annas, or Ananias, they put James, the brother of Jesus, and others to death (Acts 23).

Josephus, the Jewish historian who has given us full characteristic features of the sects in existence at the time of our Lord's birth, says that "while the Pharisees had amiable manners and cultivated concord among all, the Sadducees thought they were very boorish." While such a want of manners is not usually associated with an aristocracy, it yet describes the Sadducean cruel horseplay indulged in when Jesus was tried before an irregular meeting of the Sanhedrin (Matt. 26:67, 68). It also accounts for the shout of Ananias at Paul's trial before the same tribunal to "smite Paul on the mouth," on which occasion the Sadducees were certainly rough and overbearing (Acts 23:1–10).

Professor James Stalker in *The Ethic of Jesùs* suggests that the particular sin of the Sadducees was that of *worldliness* and that the weakness of their religious sentiment was due to that sin. Loose ideas of spiritual and eternal realities resulted in concerns of the present life. The rich fool, who pulled down his barns to build greater and was so absorbed in his property—the mere shell and husk of life—while his soul and his eternity were of no concern to him, illustrated precisely the spirit and sin of Sadducean worldliness. "Worldliness," says Professor Stalker, "stifles the very faculty of religion: and on a cold, cynical heart the appeals of religion fall like seed upon a rock."

Josephus informs us that the Sadducees had influence with the rich. On the other hand, the Pharisees, like Jesus, drew their adherents chiefly from the poor. Association with the wealthy classes caused the Sadducees to look upon money as the sign and symbol of all earthly possessions and proved that it is an enslaving power when valued and pursued for its own sake. By his statements in the Sermon on the Mount, Jesus taught that when men accumulate the apparatus of life instead of living, they become forgetful of the fact that a man's life does not consist in the abundance of the things which he possesses. "Blessed are the poor" was the opposite pole from Sadduceeism. There is one object on which the Sadducee in human nature casts itself by an inevitable instinct, and to which it clings with appalling tenacity—this is money. The teaching of Jesus is astonishingly severe regarding the heaping up of treasures on earth (Luke 6:24; Matt. 6:19, 20).

The sins of publicans, of Pharisees, of Sadducees, and of men in general were only "the outcropping above the surface of a solidarity of evil beneath the surface, which is the property of the race as a whole" and forced Jesus to level at his own generation a reiteration of invective without a parallel: "This is an evil generation . . . a generation of vipers . . . a wicked and adulterous generation." One wonders what he would have to say about human society today if he were here in the flesh and surveyed the mounting toll of crime, violence, vandalism, drug and drink and sex addiction, bloodshed, and war. Because of its corrupt state, the world is becoming ripe for another judgment similar to what it experienced in Noah's day. God loved the world, and his only begotten Son shed his blood for it because it was a world lost in sin. As the Lamb, Jesus bore away the sin of the world, but alas! so few in a "world of sinners lost, and ruined by the Fall" appropriate the emancipation from sin which he secured.

JESUS USED METAPHORS TO DESCRIBE THE HAVOC WROUGHT BY SIN

We sin when we say, do, or intend to do what we know to be alien to the will and Word of God. The term *sin* is used of anything felt, done, or said which is contrary, consciously or otherwise, to the mind of God. The word *sin* itself means a falling from or missing the right way. It also implies transgression of the law (Rom. 4:15; Heb. 10:26). The Westminster Catechism states "Sin is any want of conformity unto, or transgression of, the law of God." Sin springs in the individual man from a perverted and depraved mind. All forms of evil come "from within," said Jesus. The heart of man is the seat of impurity covering every kind of sin (Matt. 15:18, 19).

Sin is blindness. Carlyle wrote that "the beginning of a man's doom is that vision be withdrawn from him." Jesus said, "Thou blind Pharisee" (Matt. 23:26)! Then he told the Pharisees that they were "blind leaders of the blind" (Matt. 15:14) and likewise "blind guides" (Matt. 23:16, 17; see John 9:40, 41). This teaching of Jesus as to spiritual blindness corresponds to Paul's words about the mind being darkened (Rom. 1:21; 2 Cor. 3:14). Because Satan as the god of this world had blinded the minds of those who believe not, Jesus came as the light of the world.

> The whole world was lost in the darkness of sin.
> The Light of the world is Jesus.

He came that the eyes of man's darkened understanding might be enlightened, and his miracle of giving sight to those who were physically blind was a parable of what he is able to accomplish in the spiritual realm. At the commencement of his ministry, in his first sermon Jesus declared that he had come into the world for the recovering of sight to the blind, meaning, the spiritually blind, as well as those with sightless eyes (Luke 4:18). Such spiritual blindness is dark ignorance of mind, for the heart excluding the light of truth is in the blackness of midnight. John Bunyan in *Pilgrim's Progress* personifies *Ignorance* and sends him to the blackness of darkness forever. The tragedy is that men love darkness rather than light because of their evil deeds (John 1:5; 3:19; Matt. 6:23).

Sin is bondage. That a sinner is in bondage and fettered by Satan can be gathered from our Lord's teaching in his discourse on himself as the light of the world (John 8:12–50). Listening to his priceless words, the consciences of the Jews were stung as they heard him say, "Whosoever committeth sin is the slave of sin." Then came the twofold utterance: "Ye shall know *the truth,* and the truth shall make you free. . . . If *the Son* therefore shall make you free, ye shall be free indeed" (John 8:32, 36). There is no contradiction between these two statements. The one is the complement of the other, for *the Son* is *the Truth* (John 14:6), and he only, through the truth, can emancipate a sinner from the shackles of his sin and set him gloriously free (Rom. 6:14). His chains fall off, and, freed, he follows his mighty Emancipator, rejoicing in a blood-bought liberty. Charles Wesley taught the church to sing:

> Long my imprisoned spirit lay
> Fast bound in sin and nature's night;
> Thine eye diffused in quickening ray,
> I woke, the dungeon flamed with light;
> My chains fell off, my heart was free;
> I rose, went forth, and followed Thee.

There are other aspects of sin we could enlarge upon, such as the utter bankruptcy it reduces the sinner to until he becomes "full of hypocrisy and lawlessness" (Matt. 23:28), depraved like bad trees unproductive of any but rotten fruit (Matt. 7:16), destitute of faculties their sin abused (Matt. 25:28, 29), disorganization of the whole being, and with instincts perverted, fit only for "outer darkness" (Matt. 22:13). Yet running all through the teaching of Jesus about *sin* and his constant contact with sinners of all kinds is the witness that he himself was without sin. Although "made sin for us," he was never a sinner but always "separate from sinners" (2 Cor. 5:21; see 1 Pet. 2:22; 1 John 3:5).

Jesus appeared to put away sin by the sacrifice of himself, and his sinlessness gives efficacy to such a sacrifice. None could convict him of sin or find any fault in him; therefore, as the sinless Son of God, his blood is able to cleanse sinners of their sin, and transform them into saints (1 John 1:7).

> There was no other good enough
> To pay the price of sin.

He only could unlock the gate of Heaven
And let us in.

BIBLE STUDY QUESTIONS

Take time to turn to each Scripture reference and mark the verse or a portion in your Bible.

1. Explain Jesus' purpose in coming into the world.
2. Contrast publicans and sinners with the Pharisees.
3. How are the Sadducees characterized?
4. What actually is the nature of sin?

— 4 —

About Repentance

Arising out of Christ's teaching about sin is what he taught about *repentance* for sin. As we have already seen, the tragedy of human sin reveals, by contrast, the height of man's original destiny and, therefore, the necessity of a deep penitence because of his fall. More than the philosophers of his time, Jesus understood the nature and consequences of sin and thus urged upon sinners repentance toward God and faith in himself as the means of their recovery to divine favor. The terms *repent* and *Repentance* occur over twenty-five times in the four Gospels, and in the majority of references were used by Jesus. Two or three times, *repentance* is given as the watchword of the forerunner of Jesus who preached "the baptism of repentance for the remission of sins." The commencement of our Lord's ministry is described by Matthew, "From that time began Jesus to preach and to say, Repent: for the kingdom of heaven is at hand" (Matt. 4:17). Here repentance is set forth as the first aspect of Jesus' ministry.

After his choice of the twelve, Jesus commissioned them in their humbler way to begin where he did. Mark tells us that the disciples "went out and preached that men should repent." Repentance, then, in its full scriptural sense, is the sum and substance of the gospel of Jesus Christ. In his mind, the need for repentance was as universal as the fact of sin and the possibility of salvation. With utmost authority and freedom Jesus taught the sinfulness of man, but he was equally certain that sinners, even the worst, could be saved, no man having gone too far in sin as to be beyond his power to deliver. "Him that cometh to me I will in no wise cast out." The gospel hymn reminds us that "his blood can make the vilest clean."

Further, there can be no deep, genuine repentance—an essential condition of salvation—apart from the convicting ministry of the Holy Spirit revealing to the sinner the nature of his sin, not merely against himself or others, but first of all *against God* (John 16:7–11, RV). Is this not proven by our Lord's teaching in his illustration of the prodigal son who, out in the far country, "came to himself"? This phrase is equivalent to repentance in the prodigal's soul who, thus convicted, framed the repentant petition he would present to his loving father once they met again. "I have sinned against *heaven* [not first against his father, but heaven] and in thy sight, and am no more worthy to be called thy son" (Luke 15:21). When a soul is made conscious of sin by the Spirit, it is primarily of sin against God and of not having believed in him. David, in contrition, confessed, "Against thee, thee only, have I sinned" (Ps. 51:4)! Jesus taught of the Spirit's ministry: "He will reprove the world of sin . . . Of sin, because they believe not on me" (John 16:9)!

For a complete understanding of what the Master taught on the topic of *repentance,* it is essential to combine his several references to it in his seven letters to the churches (Rev. 2:3) with those to be found in the Gospels. Five of those churches received a direct call to repentance from Jesus who used several designations of himself in all seven letters.

Ephesus. This church had left (not lost) her first love and must repent and do her first works or lose her light-bearing power (Rev. 2:4, 5).

Pergamos. In this city the church had plunged into sensuality and priest-worship and was called to repent or be smitten (Rev. 2:16).

Thyatira. Alas! the church here had gone deeper into adultery and the abominable practices of the ancient Jezebel and must repent or suffer tribulation (Rev. 2:21, 22).

Sardis. Here was a church with a name to live but was spiritually dead and must repent or face judgment (Rev. 3:3).

Laodicea. This last of the seven churches was one so proud, self-righteous, and self-satisfied, with Jesus, not inside and the center and source of its life, but outside on the doorstep. This church must also repent and give Jesus his rightful place within it (Rev. 3:19).

WHAT IS REPENTANCE?

A gospel hymn simply puts it, "Repentance is to leave the sins we loved before," but while it results in such a cleavage, more is involved in contrition of soul. The word itself has several connotations. In the New Testament two words are translated *repent.* One original word means to "care afterwards," or a sorrow or remorseful regret which may lead to turning (Matt. 21:29) or which may not (Matt. 21:32), as in the case of Judas whose repentance was merely regret (Matt. 27:3). This particular word occurs six times and is twice translated in the revised version as *regret* (2 Cor. 7:8).

The second word, however, far more common and stronger in meaning, is used in all the teaching concerning repentance and is the equivalent of the Old Testament word *turn,* or *return,* one of the Hebrew terms used some six hundred times. Applied to man, then, it means turning away from sin to God (Acts 20:21) and occurs, in the noun and verb forms, some fifty-seven times. Thus, as used by Jesus, to repent implied to *turn, rightabout-face,* or go the opposite way and do the opposite thing, a turning based upon deep sorrow and remorse for and abhorrence of sin, produced by a revelation of divine holiness and hatred for sin. The three steps in this about-face are expressively set forth by David: "I thought on my ways, and I turned my feet unto thy testimonies. I made haste, and delayed not to keep thy commandments" (Ps. 119:59, 60).

At the heart of the word *repent* is the idea of *changing one's mind* for the better or to *have another mind*—the term for "mind" covering feelings, judgment, desires, and purposes. There is implied a complete reversal of the sinner's entire nature—intellectual, affectional, and moral. Repentance is a change of mind resulting in a change of life. When Martin Luther discovered, while reading his Greek Testament, that the Greek word for repentance means literally a change of mind, he experienced a great new light that revolutionized his life and service. When he discovered that biblical repentance means a change of heart, he was launched into a fierce battle against the Roman church in which he had been brought up and which he had tried to serve.

Several writers have emphasized the radical significance of the term. Archbishop Trench wrote in *The Miracles of Our Lord,* "Repentance expresses that mighty change in the mind, heart, and life wrought by the Spirit of God."

Similarly, Thomas Chalmers observed in the *International Standard Bible Encyclopedia:* "Repentance describes that deep and radical change whereby a sinner turns from the idols of sin and self unto God, and devotes every movement of the inner and outer man to the captivity of His obedience."

When Jesus told men to repent, he likewise meant the voluntary change in the mind of the sinner whereby he turns from his discovered sin (Matt. 9:12, 13). Professor Stalker in *The Ethic of Jesus* concludes his chapter on Christ's teaching concerning such a drastic change: "This was repentance: it is an upheaval of the nature from its foundations; it turns the life upside down; it is a decisive breach with the past; it is a great venture for the future."

What must be stressed, however, is that repentance, in itself, is not sufficient, and it is not salvation although it results in salvation. Repentance is only a condition of salvation and not its meritorious ground. A sinner may be a truly repentant soul, yet never know what it is to be blessedly delivered from his sin made so clear to his conscience by the Spirit of God. Penitential tears avail for nothing if they do not result in entire committal to Christ. The prodigal not only "came to himself," he also "arose and came to his father." What is the use of repentance unless we bring forth fruits worthy of such contrition (Luke 3:8)? Such expression of sorrow over sin is only profitable when it leads to remission of sins (Luke 24:47) and functions as repentance unto life.

It is not thy tears of repentance nor prayers,
But the blood that atones for the soul:
On Him then who shed it thou mayest at once
The weight of iniquities roll.

Whether repentance is a gradual movement of a convicted soul, or a sudden and complete turning away from the evil of the past life, as with Saul on that Damascus Road, it must be allied with faith if it is to result in salvation. While it is true that repentance precedes faith and brings faith and that there can be no saving faith without repentance, it is also true, in a very real sense, that repentance and faith go together and are inseparable and mutually dependent. Could anything be more concise and compelling as the message of Jesus as he went forth to preach the gospel? "Repent ye, and believe the gospel" (Mark 1:15). But such believing repentance is not a once-for-all act.

Once saved by grace through repentance and faith, the saved one must practice habitual repentance, not for the sins already blotted out by God, but for daily sins of omission and commission. John uses the continuous sense in his word of assurance, "As we keep on confessing our trespasses, the blood of Jesus keeps on cleansing us from all sin" (1 John 1:7, 9). Carlyle says, "In Repentance too is man purified. It is the grand Christian act."

When Jesus instructed his disciples in the grace of forgiveness, he said that if those who trespassed against them repented of their action, they were to be forgiven (Luke 17:3, 4). No wonder they prayed, "Lord, increase our faith"! When repentance is coupled with faith, there is always divine forgiveness for our trespasses (Matt. 6:12). True repentance, then, involves confession, contrition, and correction.

Confession (Luke 15:18). It is folly to hide anything, for God knows all the inner secrets of the heart. As the familiar features of the father looked down on the prodigal and he saw "the venerable figure, the melting eye, the gentle smile—all sunk into his heart; till, casting himself in imagination before it, he cries, 'Father, I have sinned.' "

Contrition (Luke 22:61, 62). There must be genuine grief because of sin against divine love (see Eph. 4:30). The value of repentance accompanied by confession is that it brings the sinner and the God sinned against face to face; for "the core of repentance is to recognize, not what our sinful life has been to ourselves, or even to others, but what it has been to God."

Correction (Luke 15:19). Repentance is always practical and expressed by how we act and how we live. Where necessary, amends must be made. For instance, repentance for a theft is expressed by giving back stolen property (Luke 19:7–9; see Matt. 27:3). A slanderer must retract the false statement, and an unkindness must be amended by extra kindness. Wrongdoing may be atoned for by doing better in the future. Repentance and faith are not mere sentiments, but, like hope and love, essentially practical, involving the exercise of the will to fulfill every obligation. Jeremy Taylor wrote that "true Repentance must reduce to act all its holy purposes . . . A holy life is the only perfection of Repentance."

Several of Jesus' references to repentance remind us of deep feelings of the soul that we would like to see more of in these sinful and callous days in which we live.

WHO DOES AND WHO DOES NOT REPENT?

Jesus came to call sinners to repentance (Matt. 9:13), and there is joy in heaven when the cry is heard arising from a heart smitten by conviction, "God be merciful to me a sinner" (Luke 15:7; 18:13). Sent out by the Master to preach the gospel, the disciples called upon men to repent and greatly rejoiced when they saw men sorry for their sins (Mark 6:12; Luke 10:17, 20). Two of the most incomparable illustrations of genuine repentance to be found anywhere are those given by Jesus in the parable of the prodigal and in the woman who was a sinner (Luke 15:11–32; 7:36–50).

In connection with the prodigal, Dr. Stalker in *The Christology of Jesus* says that the striking phrase, "came to himself," shows that the first element in repentance is *awakening*. He observes:

> When a man awakens out of sleep, we say he comes to himself. The Greek means literally "he entered into himself"—a remarkable phrase; for who is denoted by *he* and who by *himself*? It sounds as if in one person there are two men, the one of whom has been home but now returns. So, in common parlance, we say, a man is "out of himself," or, "beside himself," meaning that he is mad. And, indeed, sin is a brief madness; it is a drunken sleep, out of which a man has to awaken and be himself. Or "he entered himself" may suggest another line of reflection. The interior man may be conceived as a picture-gallery or corridor, hung with the scenes of one's own past, into which, in hours of leisure and reflection, one can enter and follow one's own course step by step and stage by stage.

When the prodigal was far from home, he sat down among the swine, and the past came up before him. In the cold reality of retrospect he saw everything in an entirely different light. All the glamour, excitement, and intoxication of his free life had gone; completely disillusioned, he returned home to confess, "Father, I have sinned against heaven, and in thy sight, and am no more worthy to be called thy son" (Luke 15:21). This is the kind of repentance that creates joy in heaven, and Jesus had the satisfaction of seeing many prodigals turning from their sin to him.

The other illustration the graceful pen of Luke records is that of the woman twice referred to as a sinner, the term being used in the sense of unchastity (Luke 7:37, 39). The impressive feature of the scene Luke describes is that this sinful woman never uttered a word or confessed her sin as the prodigal did. Yet from what Jesus said of this woman and of her actions, we see repentance in its purest form. To quote again from Stalker's *Ethic of Jesus:*

> Hers was a flight from a besetting sin and lost life, and in pursuit of a better life, the vision of which had risen before her eyes, that she ventured in where she dared not well be seen. There was a certain boldness in her action: but this was necessary in order to make a public break with the past. On the other hand, humility pressed her down to the earth; shame constrained her to unbind her hair and let its heavy tresses fall to hide the burning blushes; sorrow for her sins, which were many, burst in tears from her eyes. The shattering of the box of ointment may have been the final sacrifice of an instrument of her evil calling. But it would not be easy even to name all the emotions surging through her soul—timidity, admiration, gratitude, love, enthusiasm.

The eloquent silence of this sinner's repentance touched the heart of Jesus, leading him to utter some of the most beautiful sentiments, both in the parable of the creditor and the two debtors, and in his response to the woman's tears and sacrifice. Addressing Simon, he said, "Wherefore I say unto thee, her sins, which are many, are forgiven; for she loved much: but to whom little is forgiven, the same loveth little." Then came the glorious message of Jesus, thrilling the soul of this debased female and transforming her into a new creature: "He said unto her, thy sins are forgiven thee . . . Thy faith hath saved thee; go in peace" (Luke 7:48, 50).

There are many who, when deep conviction grips them and their sins come up before them, have, like the woman who was a sinner, no language but a cry. Dumb with silence, they hold their peace (Ps. 39:2). But he who is ever quick to respond to a deep recognition of guilt can read the meaning of the silence and the travail behind the tears and blesses the repentant heart with a free and full forgiveness.

There are other passages, however, in which Jesus describes the nature and the peril of those who felt there was no cause for repentance in their lives. Think of his woe pronounced on Chorazin and Bethsaida for their unconsciousness of sin. He compared them with Tyre and Sidon: "They would have repented long ago in sackcloth and ashes" (Matt. 11:20, 21; see 21:29, 32).

Cities were upbraided because they repented not, and Jesus' own generation received his judgment because it failed to repent of its sin. Nineveh repented at the preaching of Jonah, and here was a greater than the runaway prophet; yet they spurned his preaching (Matt. 12:38–42). Jesus said that there were those so hardened in sin that they would not repent if a preacher arose from the dead to preach to them (Luke 16:31). But the gracious Savior left those who were blind to their need of soul-repentance for sin. "Except ye repent, ye shall all likewise perish" (Luke 13:1–5).

Shakespeare asks:

> What then? What rests?
> Try what repentance can. What can it not?
> Yet what can it when one cannot repent?

It would seem from the teaching of Jesus that repentance is not necessary for all men, as, for instance, when he spoke of joy in heaven over one sinner that repents more than over ninety-nine just persons who need no repentance (Luke 15:7). Then he also said, "I am not come to call the righteous, but sinners to repentance" (Matt. 9:13), which is equivalent to the previous verse where Jesus chides those who think themselves sinless and in no need of repentance with the observation, "They that be whole need not a physician, but they that are sick."

In the context of these verses Jesus is dealing with two classes, namely, publicans and sinners, scribes and Pharisees. Now, he did not imply that the former certainly needed to repent; but that the latter, signified by the "ninety-nine just persons" and those who were "whole," had no need of repentance. *All* have sinned, and *all* must repent and believe if they are to be saved from their sin. Jesus knew only too well that the publicans and sinners were in dire need of repentance and that they knew they were. He also knew that of all sinners the scribes and Pharisees were the worst since they were religious hypocrites; therefore, we cannot believe he meant they had no need of repentance.

What Jesus, as the superb teacher, subtly implied was that the ninety and nine persons deemed themselves to be just and in no need of repentance, or so whole as requiring the aid of no physician. Because of their Pharisaic sins these self-righteous men required repentance far more than the "one sinner that repented" and had deeper need of divine healing than those who knew they were sick. Jesus came to call *sinners* to repentance; because the Pharisees did not deem themselves to be in such a class, he had no message for them. It was in irony, then, that Jesus referred to them as just persons with no need of repentance, for his scathing denunciations of their unjust lives as "children of the devil" reveal them to be sinners of the worst degree. Their self-righteousnesses were more filthy than the swine-smelling rags in which the prodigal returned home. Because of his repentance he exchanged his rags for the best robe in his father's house.

To summarize then, repentance, as taught by Jesus, is an evidence of the Spirit's ministry in the soul, making the contrite one conscious of his need of deliverance from besetting sins of the past. Further, the motives for Repentance are chiefly found in the goodness of God, in divine love, in the pleading desire to have sinners saved, in the inevitable consequences of sin, in the universal demands of the Gospel, and in the hope of spiritual life and membership of the kingdom of heaven (Mark 1:15; Luke 13:1–5; John 3:16; see Acts 17:30; Rom. 2:4; 1 Tim. 2:4). Attention has been drawn to the first four Beatitudes of Jesus (Matt. 5:3–6) as forming a heavenly ladder by which penitent souls pass from the domination of Satan into the kingdom of God. We have:

A consciousness of spiritual poverty dethroning pride,

A sense of personal unworthiness producing grief,

A willingness to surrender to God in genuine humility,

A strong spiritual desire developing into hunger and thirst to enter into the experience of one who wholly abandons sin and heartily turns to him who grants repentance unto life.

BIBLE STUDY QUESTIONS

Take time to turn to each Scripture reference and mark the verse or a portion in your Bible.

1. How is repentance an essential condition of salvation?
2. What is repentance?
3. In what ways is repentance expressed?
4. Who must repent? Why?

— 5 —

About Forgiveness

Since divine forgiveness is an integral part of our *salvation,* we should have included it under such a head, but as such a virtue as taught by Jesus comprises God's forgiveness of man, and man's forgiveness of man, it merits a chapter of its own. Whether used of God or man in the Gospels, the word *forgiveness* means to discharge, dismiss, acquit, let loose from, to remit a debt or sin, to pardon. It also implies giving up an inward feeling of injury or resentment, the removal of a feeling of anger and restoration for a feeling of favor and affection (see Acts 13:38, 39). The kindred terms *forgive, forgave, forgiveness* occur some forty times in the four Gospels. A peculiarity of John's Gospel is that none of these terms are found in the Authorized Version. In the Revised Version at John 20:23 *forgive* replaces "remit."

A UNIVERSAL NECESSITY

All men have need to join in the prayer, "Forgive us our debts" or trespasses, "for *all* have sinned, and come short of the glory of God." "There is none righteous, no, not one" (Rom. 3:10, 23). They have no righteousness of their own, making them acceptable to God. All have broken his laws and, therefore, require forgiveness if fellowship with him is to be restored. Jesus, who had much to say about *forgiveness,* never sought it from God simply because, as he himself confessed, "I do always those things that please [my Father]." As the sinless one, he never infringed any divine commandment and so had no cause to seek God's forgiveness. He, likewise, never had any reason to ask forgiveness of any individual because "harmless" as well as "holy" he never injured anyone while here on earth. The man after God's own heart had to write, "I will be sorry for my sin" (Ps. 38:18), but Jesus never had to say, either to God or to man, "I'm sorry for what I've done, please forgive me." All others, having sinned against God and man, require forgiveness from both. Further, divine forgiveness is of supreme importance for all who have trespassed against God, for if they die in their sin, unforgiven by God for Christ's sake, then they are forever lost. Blessed is the man whose transgression is forgiven, however, and who knows that his sin has been covered by the precious blood of Jesus (Ps. 32:1; 103:3).

A DIVINE PREROGATIVE

We may be able to forgive injuries others cause us, but only God can forgive sin. Even the carping, critical scribes realized this, for they asked, "Who can forgive sins but God only" (Mark 2:7)? They had just heard Jesus say to the palsied man whom he had healed, "Son, thy sins be forgiven thee" (Mark 2:5). What those scribes were ignorant of was that Jesus had every right and authority to forgive sins since he was God manifest in flesh. Thus, whenever Jesus forgave a sinner, he revealed his deity. More than once he made the penitent one rejoice over the gift of forgiveness.

"He said unto her, Thy sins are forgiven" (Luke 7:48).

"Thou art made whole; sin no more" (John 5:14).

"Neither do I condemn thee; go, and sin no more" (John 8:11).

Constantly, Jesus reminded his foes that as the Son of man he had power on earth to forgive sins (Matt. 9:6). To Jesus, the author of forgiveness was always God, and when he spoke of his own power to forgive sins, he always saw himself as God's representative and spokesman and medium. When they criticized him for this power, he attested his right by miracles. It was also his power to forgive sins that lent authority to his preaching and likewise declared that by his act God his Father had also forgiven the penitent. As Dr. Bond expresses it in *The Master Preacher:*

> God had revealed himself in Jesus that man might have the blessing of forgiveness personalized and applied. Through this divine right Jesus caught the ear

and heart of the sinner whom all other teachers had spurned and despised, but whom Jesus made the basis of his work. In two worlds his Word became supreme—the world of the penitent sinner and the world of the rejoicing saint.

At Calvary Jesus recognized the divine prerogative to forgive sinners when he prayed, "Father, forgive them; for they know not what they do" (Luke 23:34). In passing, it is striking that the *first* and *last* recorded sayings of Jesus begin with "Father" (see Luke 2:49; 23:46). No one else could have spoken these words, for they are utterly unlike anyone else. By *them* we understand both Jews and Gentiles, for both shared in his crucifixion (see Acts 4:26, 27). But what is meant by the words, "They know not what they do"? Jesus, speaking out of a divine consciousness, implied, "They do not know *who* it is that they are crucifying." Did not Paul substantiate this when he wrote, "Which none of the princes of this world knew: for had they known it, they would not have crucified the Lord of glory" (1 Cor. 2:8).

Christ's dying plea for the forgiveness of those humanly responsible for his death did not mean, "Take no notice, as though this sin of sins had not been committed." Had this been the implication of his prayer it would have been less than kind, for it would have been a plea for them to remain in sin and death. No, it was a supplication that God would open their eyes that they might discover the hideousness of their sin and, seeing it in its true light, might in a searching repentance, aided by God's grace, change in their hearts and seek forgiveness and restoration which the Savior longed should be theirs. While ignorance may mitigate the criminality of sin, it never exonerates it. F.W. Faber wrote:

> Jesus, Who to Thy Father prayed
> For those who all Thy Love repaid
> With this dread cup of woes—
> Teach me to conquer, Lord, like Thee,
> By patience and benignity,
> The thwarting of my foes.

In his teaching on *forgiveness,* Jesus made it plain that the exercise of such a divine prerogative to forgive depended upon the repentance of the penitent, even as the Old Testament taught. The transgressor had to admit his sorrow for sin and show that he meant to amend his ways (Josh. 24:19; Ps. 86:5; Jer. 5:1, 7). Once this had been done there was no hesitation on God's part to forgive (1 Kings 8:36, 56; Ps. 103:3). Thus, in his instruction in the art of forgiving, twice over Jesus said, "If he repent, forgive him" (Luke 17:3, 4). It has ever been his nature to forgive, but first those requiring his forgiving grace must repent (Luke 18:13; see Ezek. 33:11; Hos. 14:1). Without genuine repentance for sin there can be no divine forgiveness. Jesus went on to declare that within this condition no limit should be put on forgiveness even though it is required "until seventy times seven" (Matt. 18:21–35), a phrase meaning endlessly, or so often as it may be required.

Peter went beyond the current generosity of his day in respect to the limit of forgiveness. God denounced punishment on Damascus, Tyre, and Judah, in a formula always beginning, "For three transgressions of . . . and for four" (Amos 1, 2). This suggests that the nations had concluded in four transgressions the limit of forgiveness, but Peter went one better and asked if *seven times* would be the limit of forgiveness the Savior would approve. What Peter had to learn was that "forgive" means *forthgive,* that is, to *dismiss* absolutely from thought. Jesus suggests that he who really forgives does not keep count of the offenses pardoned. Some say they forgive but cannot forget. But they do not forgive if they do not forget, so far as any resentful memory is concerned. As Peter found it hard to enter into the spirit of this grace, Jesus added a parable to show our infinite obligation to forgive.

There had to be at all times the cultivation of the spirit of forgiveness, but only on the basis of repentance and confession. If we have not this spirit, then God will not hear or heed our prayers. Is this not the spirit Tennyson exhorts us to manifest:

> O Man, forgive thy mortal foe,
> Nor ever strike him blow for blow;
> For all the souls on earth that live
> To be forgiven must forgive—
> Forgive him seventy times and seven:
> For all the blessed souls in Heaven
> Are both Forgivers and Forgiven.

There is one sin, however, Jesus said a forgiving God cannot forgive. It is blasphemy against the Holy Spirit, known as the *unpardonable sin,* reference to which is found under the section, "About the Holy Spirit." Mark calls this "the eternal sin" (Matt. 12:31, 32; Mark 3: 28–30). For this particular sin, the sinner can never have forgiveness (Mark 3:29). The solemn words of Jesus regarding this tragic state were uttered after his clash with the Pharisees and in them he was referring to a condition of soul the Pharisees manifested by their words, actions, and attitude. As James N. Dow puts it in his *Gem Dictionary of the Bible:*

> In life their souls were dead; they were completely impervious to the influence of the Holy Spirit. Such a soul cannot possibly find its way back to the beginning and start again. It is, in fact, dead. God cannot forgive such a soul for such a soul is unable to receive and appreciate forgiveness. It has gone too far ever to return.

A HUMAN OBLIGATION

It will be further found that in his teaching Jesus emphasized the relationship between the two aspects of forgiveness, namely, God's forgiveness of man, and man's forgiveness of man. Passages like the following are most emphatic in this warning:

"If ye forgive men their trespasses, your heavenly Father will also forgive you: But if ye forgive not men their trespasses, neither will your Father forgive your trespasses" (Matt. 6:14–15).

"Forgive, and ye shall be forgiven" (Luke 6:37).

"Likewise shall my heavenly Father do also unto you, if ye from your hearts forgive not every one his brother their trespasses" (Matt. 18:35).

With this teaching of his Lord in mind, Paul likewise relates the two phases of forgiveness when writing to the Ephesians: "Forgiving one another, even as God for Christ's sake hath forgiven you" (Eph. 4:32). In two Parables, namely, the two debtors and the prodigal son (Matt. 18:21–35; Luke 15:11–24), Jesus sets forth the same related phases of forgiveness.

> Return my son,
> To thy Redeemer!—Died He not in love!—
> The sinless, the Divine, the Son of God—
> Breathing Forgiveness 'midst all agonies;
> And *We,*—dare we be ruthless?

At the heart of the teaching of Jesus then was the insistence that the human who would not forgive the human could never be forgiven of God. Nothing of this kind had been conceived in the world before, and Jesus enforced it in his parable about those who, having a proper estimate of the greatness of the forgiveness extended to themselves, would find it too difficut not to forgive—even their enemies. Forgive meant they would be compelled by love to forgive. Mutual forgiveness indicates the condition of the heart accepting divine forgiveness with humility. Both in the Lord's Prayer and in his instruction to Peter, Jesus seems to say, "How dare you ask God to forgive you when you refuse your forgiveness to a brother?"

God's forgiveness involves the restoration of happy relationships, but this is impossible if his children continue to harbor toward each other a spirit which is so much out of harmony with the spirit of him with whom is forgiveness that he might be feared. We must do to others as we wish God to do to us; if we refuse to forgive, our own forgiveness is denied (Matt. 18:21–35). If he was unwilling to forgive us, as we are to forgive those who offend us, we would never be saved. Forgiven himself, Stephen illustrated in his martyrdom how to emulate the divine example (Acts 7:60). Jesus made the forgiving spirit an antecedent to prayer, "When ye stand praying, forgive, if ye have ought against any" (Mark 11:25). This is what Stephen did. It would seem as if Jesus deemed an unforgiving spirit to be one of the most heinous of sins. As God sets the example of ready clemency, the child ought to imitate the Father (Matt. 5:45). Great stress is laid on forgiving injuries, of which Jesus cited three kinds: injury to the person (Matt. 5:39); loss of property (Matt. 5:40); defamation of character (Matt. 5:11).

Ever practical, Jesus gave instructions as to the steps to be taken in securing reconciliation, beginning with a private session to talk things over (Matt. 18:15–17). Every effort must be made to win the wrongdoer to repentance, and only when he has exhausted every effort may the effort be abandoned. The object of the brother seeking the restoration of his fellow believer is that of gaining him for the truth. The word *ought* Jesus constantly used is the Greek form of the verb for "owe." If forgiven by him, we are debtors to others in that we must manifest toward them the same magnanimity. "How much owest thou unto my Lord" (Luke 16:5)? We cannot measure the debt of gratitude we owe him for the forgiveness of our sins and then the debt we must discharge toward those who sin against us. Does not the sentiment of Longfellow make a fitting conclusion to the teaching and example of Jesus regarding the grace of forgiveness?

> . . . Why shouldest thou hate then thy Brother?
> Hateth he thee?—Forgive! For 'tis sweet to stammer one letter
> Of the Eternal's language;—on earth it is called *Forgiveness.*
> Knowest thou Him?—Who forgave, with the Crown of Thorns on His temples!
> Earnestly praying for His foes, for His murderers,—say dost thou know *Him?*
> Ah! thou confessest His name, so follow likewise His example!

BIBLE STUDY QUESTIONS

Take time to turn to each Scripture reference and mark the verse or a portion in your Bible.

1. What does forgiveness mean?

2. Discuss why Jesus never asked the Father for forgiveness.
3. How could Jesus forgive sins?
4. What is man's part in forgiveness?

— 6 —

About Salvation

In the purpose of God, repentance should result in salvation. Made conscious of his need as a sinner, the repentant one must be brought to see the Savior, hanging on the tree for his emancipation from the thralldom of past sin and as his guarantee that sin shall not again have dominion over him. When the keeper of the prison was smitten with conviction by the manifestation of divine power in the great earthquake that shook the prison to its foundations, he came trembling before Paul and Silas, and cried, "Sirs, what must I do to be saved?" And the miracle happened, for the jailer rejoiced and believed in God with all his house (Acts 16:25–34).

That *salvation* was a topic dear to the heart of him who came to save is evident from the many references to it in his oral ministry. Jesus used the term *to save* about twenty-seven times; and *salvation* twice. The meaning of these evangelical terms is "integral in all his teaching, and is illustrated by his whole ministry." Dr. Graham Scroggie goes on to say in *A Guide to the Gospels* that "salvation is a central idea in which others meet, such as sin, repentance, faith, regeneration, justification, life, righteousness, and it stands in contrast to the ideas of lost, destruction, perish and death." The salvation Jesus came to provide for the lost he illustrated in his parables of the Pharisee and the publican, the lost sheep, the good shepherd, the good Samaritan, the great supper, and the wedding feast.

Before devoting ourselves to a study of what Jesus taught regarding the topic of *salvation,* it is necessary to take notice of three related terms he used and which in evangelical parlance are deemed to signify the same spiritual experience of a sinner when his is a heartfelt sorrow for sin, namely, *conversion, regeneration,* and *justification.* That these are not simply different words describing the initial work of grace in the soul is evident from an examination of them..

CONVERSION

Three times Jesus used the word *convert* in three different ways. First, it spoke of the character of his mission, "Lest at any time . . . they should be converted and I should heal them" (Matt. 13:15; Mark 4:12; John 12:40). In the second he employed the word in his teaching on humility, "Except ye be converted, and become as children" (Matt. 18:3). Then there is the reference to Peter's fall and recovery, "When thou art converted, strengthen thy brethren" (Luke 22:32).

In gospel crusades, numbers are given of *converts,* their "conversion" being reckoned as tantamount to their full surrender to the claims of Christ. But Peter was not one who needed a conversion of this order, for he was both a disciple and an apostle already and called *blessed* by Jesus because of his confession of his master's messiahship and deity. What, then, did Jesus mean when he said to Peter, "When thou art converted"? The word *convert* itself means to turn again. Peter, in his denial, followed Jesus afar off or turned away from him; so there came the assurance that when he had turned back to his forsaken Lord again, he would be able to forewarn others.

Conversion, then, is a human act and one that can be repeated many times. A truly regenerated person may backslide, but under the impulse of the Spirit slides back or returns to the Lord. When Jesus called those who were his chosen ones to be "converted," he was teaching them a lesson on the necessity of lowliness of heart and that, although grown men, they must turn back again to childlike innocency, trust, and guilelessness. Under conviction, a person may turn toward the Savior, "Turn thou me" (Jer. 31:18), but if the turned one is to be healed, the turning must result in faith and surrender.

Conversion is the movement of the soul toward grace; regeneration is the infusion of that grace within the soul. The sinner must be converted *unto the Lord* (Ps. 51:13). After an evangelistic campaign many of the so-called converts are seen and heard of no more or they may journey for awhile on the Christian pathway then disappear because, as Jesus put it in his parable of the sower, they do not have the *root* in themselves (Matt. 13:21). Their conversion is proven to be merely external, consisting only of a temporary profession. *Conversion* is the motion of the creature toward God, but *regeneration* is the motion of God within the creature whereby he becomes a new creature of creation, in Christ Jesus. Conversion is a human act, and one that can be repeated, but regeneration is a divine act that once accomplished can never occur again. "Whatsoever God doeth, it shall be for ever" (Eccles. 3:14).

REGENERATION

This term occurs only twice in the New Testament and in each case implies a *re-creation.* When our Lord said, "Ye which have followed me in the regeneration" (Matt. 19:28), he was referring to the re-creation of the social order and to the renewal of the earth when his kingdom comes (Isa. 11:6–9; Rom. 8:19–22). But when Paul used the same word in writing of "the washing of regeneration" (Titus 3:5), he was speaking of the new birth of a convicted, believing person born anew, "not of blood, nor the will of the flesh, nor of the will of man, but of God" (John 1:13). Through such a re-creation, the sinner becomes a son of God (John 1:12).

While Jesus did not use this evangelical term *regeneration* of a believing person, all that it represents in this connection was fully taught by him in his memorable night conversation with Nicodemus when he uttered his fiat: "Ye must be born again [or born anew]" (John 3:7). Man is born in sin and must be reborn if he is to enter the kingdom of heaven. "Except a man be born again—born from above—he cannot see the kingdom of heaven" (John 3:3). As the result of his departure from God, man became degenerated, and in order for him to be restored to fellowship with God he must be *re*generated. Comparing conversion with regeneration and other works of grace, we have these differences:

Conversion is our turning to the Lord; regeneration, his turning unto us to bring us into sonship.

Conversion is the expression of longing for life eternal; regeneration is the impartation of this life.

Further, regeneration differs from *adoption* in that the latter entitles us to heaven, while the former is a guarantee of heavenly bliss. Then there is the distinction between *justification* and *regeneration*—the former acquitting us from the charge of guilt, being effected by the obedience, death, and resurrection of Jesus; the latter being the work of the Holy Spirit. Comparison between these two acts of grace must be carefully defined.

Regeneration does not justify, nor does justification regenerate, although there cannot be the one without the other (see Titus 3:5–7). They are separate and distinct from each other in every respect, but inseparable, both occurring at the same time by the same act of faith. Justification cancels the guilt of the repentant sinner. Regeneration imparts a new nature, a spiritual resurrection into a new life. Other ways of expressing differences are as follows:

Regeneration is a change of nature; justification is pardon for sin.

Regeneration is a work done *within us;* justification is work done for us.

Regeneration is a change of *character;* justification is a change of *relationship.*

Regeneration shows God as *creator,* or *life-giver;* adoption shows him as a *loving Father.*

Justification leads us to think of him as a righteous yet merciful *Judge;* forgiveness reveals him as a sovereign or king, cancelling the past violation of his law.

At this point, a word or two may be fitting concerning God's act in declaring a person righteous and altogether free from the demands and penalty of his broken law.

JUSTIFICATION

This act or decree of God made in heaven whereby he alone declares a believing sinner righteous through the merits of a substitute was surely in the mind of Jesus in his parable of the Pharisee and the publican who went up to the Temple to pray (Luke 18:9–14). The Pharisee was at pains to justify himself, even as Jesus revealed more when he condemned the Pharisees as a whole for justifying themselves before men (Luke 16:15). Likewise the lawyer with whom Jesus dealt was "willing to justify himself" (Luke 10:29). But with the repentant, abased publican, it was different, for like other publicans he "justified God" (Luke 7:29). In contrast to the Pharisee, the publican had no righteousness of his own, no fasting, no tithing to present as a plea. The Pharisee prayed with *himself,* but the distressed publican, so smitten with contrition, would not lift up so much as his eyes to heaven. All that he could do was to cry in agony, "God, be merciful to me a sinner" (Luke 18:13).

The remarkable feature about this prayer that Jesus put into the lips of the publican is that the word *merciful* is that used of "the blood-sprinkled mercy-seat" (Lev. 16:5) and of "propitiation," Paul's great term (Rom. 3:25). So, as Dr. C. I. Scofield suggests, his prayer might be paraphrased, "Be toward me as thou art when thou lookest upon the atoning blood." This was why, as Jesus put it, "This man went down to his house justified *rather* than the other" (Luke 18:14). In this sentence Jesus declares a sinner righteous before God because of the substitutionary act of another. As the Westminster Catechism expresses it,

> Justification is an act of God's free grace wherein He pardoneth all our sins, and accepteth us as righteous in His sight, only for the righteousness of Christ imputed to us and received by faith alone.

Allied to this justification is *reconciliation* whereby enmity is exchanged for friendship (see Rom. 5:10, 11, margin). As the judge, God pardons and justifies; as the Father, he forgives and reconciles. In the evangelical realm, *justification* becomes ours by:

God (Rom. 3:26; 4:5; 8:33).
Christ (Gal. 2:16).
Grace freely (Rom. 3:24; Gal. 2:16).
Faith (Gal. 3:8).
His blood (Rom. 5:9).
His knowledge (Isa. 53:11).

All the gospel truths we have just mentioned are wrapped up in salvation, a topic so prominent in the teaching of Jesus.

SALVATION

Before Jesus became man, he knew how sin had left its serpent's trail upon men and that divine wrath rested upon a world of sinners; and it was because he heard the wail of the lost and as God the son was manifested in flesh, that all flesh might be saved. This is why that when we come to consider his ministry we find that in his teaching, *sin* and *salvation* were complementary terms, the prevalence of the former carrying with it the possibility of the latter. Jesus came into a lost world, died, and rose again that abounding sin might give way to the more abundant salvation and grace.

Entering his brief but dynamic mission, Jesus caught up the slogan of John, his forerunner, *Repent ye!* and proclaimed it. In his thinking and teaching the need for repentance was as universal as the fact of sin and the provision of salvation.

Although he declared that "God so loved the world," he did not generalize in his teaching, which was always based on individualism. In his thought, the individual was the unit of salvation, as evidenced by his "whosoevers." We hear and read a great deal today about a social salvation and about the utopia of an ideal republic. But the individual is forgotten.

Jesus, however, came as an individual Savior to preach an individual evangel. This is why the bulk of his wonderful topics were presented to individuals and why he directed his appeal to the conscience of each person. Jesus made real the republic of God to each individual believer in whose heart and life the forces of good became operative and dominant. The simple heart of one man or woman gave him suitable audience. Fresh from his own heart, these truths came into the individual life of select men and women, creating new ideals and hopes and forming new character and destiny, as Nicodemus, the woman at the well, and others experienced.

The embodiment of salvation. In consideration of such a glorious, evangelical theme, it is important at the outset to realize that salvation is not *something* but *someone.* "Behold, God is my salvation." When godly, aged Simeon took up the child Jesus in his arms and looked at his sweet, innocent face, he said, "Lord, now lettest thou thy servant depart in peace, according to thy word: For mine eyes have seen the salvation" (Luke 2:29, 30). Having seen salvation personified in him who was born a Savior, Simeon wanted to go to heaven. Salvation, then, is not merely a spiritual gift that Jesus offers; it is *himself*

Further, his mission to save is embodied in his human name *Jesus,* which means, "Jehovah the Savior" (Matt. 1:21). Used as an acrostic, this peerless name spells our salvation:

J esus
E ternally
S aves
U s
S inners

Call Him Jesus! He shall save us
From the tyranny of sin;
From its condemnation save us,
From iniquity within.

The doctrine of salvation. What, exactly, is the nature of this gift the giver is in himself? When Jesus said to Zacchaeus, "Today is salvation come to this house," it actually came in his person. Then he pronounced in no uncertain terms why he left the glory and took upon himself frail flesh. "The Son of man is come to seek and to save that which was lost" implied that Zacchaeus was one of the sinners in deep need of salvation (Luke 19:7, 9, 10). But what constituted such a salvation for this rich, prominent tax gatherer? It meant his recovery as a fallen man, from a state of sin and unbelief, his deliverance from condemnation and guilt, and his restoration to divine favor and holiness. No wonder Zacchaeus received Jesus joyfully!

Redemption is God's provision for man's emancipation from iniquity; *salvation* is the bringing about or realization of such a deliverance. The former is like making and equipping a lifeboat, while the latter is like being rescued by means of a lifeboat. Salvation, or being saved, in its evangelical sense signifies the work the Savior at once accomplishes in and for the sinner who yields to him, and it includes forgiveness or pardon, regeneration, justification, and adoption. The list of our salvation rights is formidable as a study of relevant passages reveals. Suffice it to say that Jesus, by his finished work at Calvary, can save all who believe from Satan and all his works (see Matt. 18:11). This was the truth Nicodemus learned from the lips of Jesus, namely, that *redemption* is the basis of regeneration and that a new creation is only possible through the precious blood. Listening to Jesus as he spoke of the necessity of a rebirth, the master of Israel asked, "How can these things be?" Then Jesus said only through his being lifted up to die upon the cross as the manifestation of God's love for a lost world (John 3:9–16).

The necessity of salvation. Because all men are sinners, Jesus came not to destroy them but to save them, not only from present sin, but from eternal destruction which would be theirs if they died in their sin. From his remarkable teaching given to the woman at the well, it would seem as if those of his own nation were only those in dire need of salvation, for Jesus said, "Salvation is of the Jews" (John 4:22). Godet, however, translates this phrase as "Because salvation comes from the Jews," meaning that through them salvation was to come to the world. Jesus himself, who came as the Savior of the world, was a Jew, and his apostles, who were so wonderfully used in the salvation of multitudes in the early days of the church, were Jews. "It was at Jerusalem that the living God has made himself known: and that it is by means of the Jews that he intends to give salvation to the world."

Both Jews and Gentiles are born in sin, for the whole world is guilty before God, and *all* have sinned and come short of his glory and must be saved if they are to escape eternal woe for their sin. It is thus that Jesus, in himself, is the only light to lighten the Gentiles and the only glory of his people Israel (Luke 2:32). The jailer recognized the necessity of salvation when he cried, "What *must* I do to be saved?' But Paul had an immediate answer, "Believe on the Lord Jesus Christ, and thou shalt be saved" (Acts 16:30, 31). Would that the masses of godless men and women today could be made conscious of the imperative need of God's matchless saving grace and power (Luke 3:6).

The conditions of salvation. As used here *condition* means something necessary to, yet not the cause of, a certain result. God is willing and able to save sinners, but there are things they must do before the gift of salvation becomes theirs. What is the use of his being the horn of salvation (Luke 1:69) unless we appropriate him as such and drink out of such a horn? If, as Jesus said, he is "the door," and it is only as we enter into him that we can be saved, then it is useless to stand outside the door. Entrance is the condition of salvation (John 10:9).

If he is "the Truth," then it is only as we receive his testimony that we can be saved (John 5:34).

The *first* condition of salvation is *repentance,* which, as we have already shown, involves a deep conviction of sin when the penitent one sees himself to be guilty of sin before God and deserving of punishment. Unless there is contrition for sin, and the willingness to renounce a sinful past coupled with a full confession of sin to God, the salvation he offers cannot be given. All of this is what Jesus taught in his parable of the prodigal son.

The *second* condition is *faith,* the only ground or foundation of which is the death and resurrection of Jesus. While repentance and faith are the conditions required of the sinner who would be saved (Mark 1:15), the procuring cause of salvation is the redeeming work of Christ (John 3:16). "He that believeth on the Son hath everlasting life" (John 3:36). When a sinner is urged to exercise faith in Christ for salvation, and says he cannot believe, he must be reminded that even the faith, like the salvation, is the gift of God (Eph. 2:8). God gives to all the power to believe, but the act of believing is the sinner's own, just as the power to walk is God's gift, though walking is man's own act.

Faith, which is belief or trust, may be either faith with understanding, often called "intellectual faith," or faith in action, referred to as "practical faith" or "heart faith." *Intellectual faith* is believing some*thing* with the mind; *Heart faith* is the act of trusting some*one.* A sick man exercises the former kind when he believes that his doctor is able to cure or relieve him; he manifests the latter kind when he trusts or commits himself to the doctor's advice and treatment. In his parable of the sower, Jesus spoke of the Devil taking the word out of the hearts of those who hear it, "lest they should believe [with their hearts] and be saved" (Luke 8:12). It is possible to believe with the mind all the Bible says, yet lack saving faith. The demons, James described, had intellectual faith, for they believed what the Bible taught—and trembled—but were unable to manifest saving faith (James 2:19).

The woman who was a sinner, and who by her actions displayed contrition and repentance, revealed *intellectual faith,* for she knew who Jesus was, and also *saving faith,* for he said to her, "Woman, thy faith hath saved thee" (Luke 7:50). Saving faith, then, is that act of personal heart-trust by which the sinner commits himself to God and accepts as his own the salvation God so freely offers. Blind Bartimaeus was another who exercised both kinds of faith and had the joy of hearing Jesus say, "Thy faith hath made thee whole" (Mark 10:52; see 9:23, 24).

It would seem as if Jesus added a *third* condition for salvation, for when he commissioned his disciples to go out into all the world and preach the gospel to every creature, he said, "He that believeth *and is baptized* shall be saved" (Mark 16:16). This does not imply that if a sinner repents of his sin and by faith accepts Christ as his personal Savior, yet fails to be baptized, that he is not saved, for Paul distinctly says, "By grace are ye saved through faith" (Eph. 2:8). If baptism is essential to salvation then the dying thief who repented and believed, was not saved. Barnes in his *New Testament* commentary explains:

> Jesus did not say that a man *could not* be saved without baptism, but he has strongly implied that where this is neglected, *knowing it to be a command of the Saviour,* it endangers the salvation of the soul. *Faith* and *Baptism* are the beginnings of a Christian life; the one the beginning of piety *in the soul,* the other of its manifestation *before men,* or a profession of religion.

The sacrament of baptism provides an outward and visible sign of inward grace and represents the grafting into the body of the regenerated one. Baptism by immersion portrays identification with Christ in his death, burial, and resurrection (see 1 Cor. 12:13; Rom. 6:3–10; Col. 2:12). While not an essential condition to salvation, baptism is essential to obedience to Jesus who left us an example in his own baptism that we should follow his steps. Throughout the early church, baptism was an accompaniment of salvation. The rite of baptism practiced by John the Baptist was a baptism unto repentance, but Jesus who was baptized by John had no sin to repent of. Nevertheless, his act identified him with those he had come to save. With him, baptism was a symbol of self-dedication in purity of heart to the service of God, the symbols of the dove and the voice assuring Jesus that the Spirit of the Lord was upon him as he commenced his great task as the Savior of the world.

The tenses of salvation. Phrases like "abundant salvation," "full salvation," "save to the uttermost" (Heb. 7:25), imply developing phases, aspects, or tenses of salvation. A simple hymn expresses it:

Jesus saves me all the time,
Jesus saves me now.

Did he himself not say, "He that endureth unto the end shall be saved"? (Matt. 10:22; 24:13, 22). Jesus came to provide, not only life, but life more abundant (John 10:10). We must not limit salvation to what is accomplished when, in the hour of decision for Christ, we received him as our personal Savior. This evangelical term has a wider meaning, signifying a daily and full deliverance from sin and its consequences, until redeemed in soul *and body,* we are taken into heaven. A drowning man at sea is *saved* when pulled into a lifeboat, but in a fuller sense his salvation includes a daily recovery from exhaustion and injury, the necessity of food and clothing, and conveyance to and housing on shore. So a sinner is *saved* when forgiven and accepted by God; in another sense he is *being saved* all the time until *finally saved* in heaven. Thus a believer is one

Who has been saved—*Past:* Penalty of Sin.

Is being saved—*Present:* Power of Sin.

Has yet to be saved—*Prospective:* Presence of sin.

Paul, who was deeply immersed in all the topics the Master taught, and who is still the unrivaled expositor of them, dearly loved the doctrine of salvation Jesus proclaimed. As a servant of the most high God, Paul lived only to declare the way of salvation, which he did with marvelous results. This Christ-honoring apostle rings the changes on the three tenses of salvation in his Roman Epistle.

Past tense. In verses Romans 1:14–16, Paul gives us a trio of *I am's,* the last being, "I am not ashamed of the gospel of Christ: for it is the power of God unto salvation to every one that believeth." Salvation, then, is a gift we receive the moment we accept, by faith, the Lord Jesus as our personal Savior. This is a salvation from *the penalty of sin.* Convicted by the Holy Spirit of our sin, and of our consequent condemnation, for "the soul that sinneth it shall die," and through our reception of the crucified, risen Lord, our guilty past was blotted out. Then came the assurance that God would remember our sins against us no more forever, and so reconciled to God through the Savior, we were able to sing:

> 'Tis done, the great transaction's done,
> I am my Lord's, and He is mine.

Thereafter, we could confess, "Praise God, I am saved!" Yes, and once saved in this way, we are saved forever, for such a salvation embracing regeneration, justification, and adoption can never be repeated. One may lose the joy of such a salvation for a little, but never the divinely wrought salvation itself, for we have been saved with "an everlasting salvation in the Lord," as Isaiah expresses it. This, therefore, is the initial feature of the salvation so freely offered to the sinner, the reception of which blots out his past sins.

For nothing can untwine
Thy life from mine.

Present tense. When God saves a person and banishes the guilt behind him, he does not take away from him any possibility of sinning. The old nature is not eradicated but remains. The believing sinner, however, is made the recipient of a new nature, hence the constant conflict Paul reminds us of in the phrase, "When *I* [saved Paul] would do good, evil [the old Saul of Tarsus] is with me." The *penalty* of sin, associated with the past, has been banished, but the *power* of sin remains, and thus salvation is necessary from the government of sin and is promised in the declaration of victory. "Sin shall not have dominion over you." So, although I can say, "I have been saved," I can also say, "I am being saved." This is the salvation we show forth day by day in victory over the world, the flesh, and the Devil.

But how is this daily salvation made possible? In the fifth chapter of Romans, we have a remarkable passage, the import of which all too few saved sinners understand. "For if, when *we were* enemies, we were reconciled to God by the death of his Son"—salvation in its past tense, a salvation effected by the sacrifice of the cross—"much more, *being* reconciled [or being saved], we *shall be saved* by his life" (Rom. 5:10). Here we have a twofold salvation—one by *his death,* the other by *his life.* This latter aspect cannot refer to Christ's earthly life. We hear a good deal about living like Jesus, but there is no salvation through mere imitation. No, the words, *his life,* refer to his present life, his risen, glorified, throne life in heaven. Because he is alive forever more and all power has been given unto him, he is able to save us moment by moment from sin's seductive snares. Appropriating his risen life, we can be more than conquerors. The question then is, Although saved, are we being saved?

Love's resistless current sweeping
All the regions deep within,
Thought, and wish, and senses keeping
Now, and *every instant,* clean
Full salvation!
From the guilt and power of sin.

Prospective tense. Blessedly saved and continuously saved, we yet live in a sinful world with its insistent temptation to sin. Saved from the *penalty* of sin and daily saved from the *power* of sin, we need to be saved from the *presence* of sin and such an aspect has been provided in him who is our salvation. Dealing with the return of Jesus for those saved by grace, Paul reminds us that if we can read the signs of the time, then we must bestir ourselves from spiritual lethargy, for "Now is our salvation *nearer* than when we believed" (Rom. 13:11). Did we not receive salvation when we first believed? Yes. Do we not receive salvation as we keep on believing? Yes. Then what salvation is this Paul says is *nearer*? The answer is that Jesus who in himself is our salvation is nearer the rapture than when we received him as our Savior.

When he does "appear the second time without

sin unto salvation," he will gather his truly saved ones around him and remove them from the entire presence of sin. Then, "the church will be saved to sin no more." Receiving us unto himself he will translate us to a sinless world in which we shall be perfectly holy and in no further need of salvation. What a great salvation God has provided us with, and because it was purchased at such tremendous cost, and confers so many blessings to cover our past, present, and future, we dare not neglect it (Heb. 2:3). For sinners who deliberately neglect it, there is no escape. Escape from what? Jesus warned sinners against the eternal condemnation if they died in their sin, rejecting his proffered salvation (John 8:24).

BIBLE STUDY QUESTIONS

Take time to turn to each Scripture reference and mark the verse or a portion in your Bible.

1. Compare and contrast conversion, regeneration, and justification.
2. What is salvation and what does it include?
3. What conditions accompany salvation?
4. Discuss briefly the three tenses of salvation.

— 7 —

About Righteousness

All the truths enunciated by Jesus were, first of all, experienced by him who came as the personification of truth. "I am . . . the Truth." Thus, when he exhorted those around him to "search the Scriptures," meaning, of course, the Old Testament portion of the Bible, he was only urging others to do something he had daily joy in doing. He was able to expound unto his disciples in *all* the Scriptures the things concerning himself because his mind was saturated with every phase of truth they presented. The virtue we are now to deal with is a case in point, for *righteousness*, divine and human, pervades the Old Testament, and Jesus knew it to be one of its most prominent ideas.

In the Gospels, Jesus is before us as one with a passion for righteousness which may be called "a peculiarly Hebrew instinct." In his Sermon on the Mount, *righteousness* is seen to be one of the elements of blessedness, for after expounding his Beatitudes, Jesus returns to *righteousness* and makes it the text of his ensuing discourse. His characteristic phrase, "Hungering and thirsting after righteousness," is but another way of saying, "Blessed is he that doeth righteousness" (Ps. 106:3). Jesus not only "preached righteousness to the congregation," he was the paragon of such a virtue. Although in Bible usage *justification* is the act of pronouncing one righteous, seeing the literal root of the word *justification* is to "make righteous," *righteousness* as used by Jesus not only implied this significance but also included rightness according to the divine standard, or conformity to the will and nature of God himself.

From our Lord's teaching on *righteousness* both its religious and practical aspects are emphasized. Not only was it a term he used for the behavior of man to man, but also one indicating the prize of the favorable verdict of God on a man's character and conduct. Through grace, made righteous, the believer must live and act righteously. The root idea of *righteousness* is "right"—right before God and right before men—and it is used this way by Jesus (Matt. 20:4–7; Luke 12:57). Whoever is right with God is, or should be, righteous in all his ways. It has been pointed out that in the teaching of Jesus the word *righteousness* and its cognates are also translated *just,* five times (e.g., Matt. 5:45); *righteous,* eighteen times (e.g., Luke 5:32); *justify,* four times (e.g., Matt. 11:19); *judge,* once (e.g., Luke 12:14); *righteousness,* eight times (e.g., John 16:8, 10).

It is from these various terms Jesus used that we are able to discover that righteousness embraces *morality,* or man's relation to men, and *religion,* or man's relation to God.

GOD IS THE ABSOLUTE RIGHTEOUSNESS

Absolute in *holiness,* God cannot be anything else but absolute in righteousness. Jesus called God, *righteous Father,* a term corresponding to the Old Testament revelation of his righteousness, "The righteous God" (Ps. 7:8, 11). "The Lord God of Israel is righteous" (Ezra 9:15). This also coincides with the Pauline phrase, "The righteousness of God" (2 Cor. 5:21; Phil. 3:8, 9). As the source and sum of righteousness, God is just and righteous in all his ways, as Jesus often confirmed.

CHRIST WAS ALWAYS RIGHT IN HIS JUDGMENT OF ALL THINGS

Had he not been the sinless one, Jesus' claim, "My judgment is just [or righteous]" (John 5:30), would have been arrogant assumption. To him, righteousness meant being *right* in all things, God-ward and manward. Jesus fulfilled *all* righteousness and urged *all* to follow him in such a virtue (Matt. 3:15). God made him to be our *righteousness,* and actually the "righteousness of God" *is* Christ, not his obedience to the Father, but himself (1 Cor. 1:30). Righteousness then is not only a policy and mode of practice but a *person,* and we become the righteousness of God in him (2 Cor. 5:21). As the righteous one, Jesus alone can make a sinner right with God, as he is made righteous by faith (Rom. 4:3; Gal. 3:6). Those who are *right* have repented of their sins (Matt. 9:13).

Isaiah spoke of the Lord clothing him with "the

robe of righteousness" (Isa. 61:10), and when Paul speaks about "putting on the Lord Jesus Christ" (Rom. 13:14), he infers that the believer is one who is clothed with divine righteousness. Count Zinzendorf expresses this wonderful truth in his great hymn on such righteousness:

> Jesus, Thy blood and righteousness
> My beauty are, my glorious dress;
> Midst flaming worlds, in these arrayed,
> With joy shall I lift up my head.
>
> His spotless robe the same appears,
> When ruined nature sinks in fears;
> No age can change its glorious hue;
> Its glory is for ever new.

THE HOLY SPIRIT CAME TO CONVINCE THE WORLD OF WHAT WAS RIGHT

In his teaching concerning the threefold work of the Holy Spirit toward the world, Jesus said when the Spirit came, as he did at Pentecost as the gift of the Father and of the Son, that he would convict the world "of sin, of righteousness, of judgment" (John 16:8–11).

It will be noted that Jesus gave righteousness the middle position, or as the intermediate one between the two others, signifying, as Godet observes, "*righteousness* applying itself to *sin* to produce *judgment*." Ever since Pentecost the Spirit has been active, convicting sinful and unjust men of the necessity of the new birth to make them holy and righteous. To quote Godet again:

Thus by the testimony of the Spirit the world, righteous in its own eyes, will be declared sinful; the condemned malefactor will be proved righteous; and the true author of this crime will receive his irrevocable sentence. Such are the three ideas contained in this passage, whose powerful originality it is impossible not to recognize.

HUMANITY IS DIVIDED INTO TWO CLASSES

A distinctive feature of the teaching of Jesus was his way of classifying different types of men. For instance, he described those who were *wrong* (Matt. 23:28, 29, 35), and those who were *right* (Matt. 5:45; 13:17, 41, 43. Men may not like these clearly defined classes; yet they are in one or the other group. Further, Jesus spoke of *right* as a virtue implying *wrong.* All householders were not righteous, but Jesus, as the perfect hirer of laborers for his vineyard, assures them, "Whatsoever is right I will give you . . . Whatsoever is right, that shall ye receive" (Matt. 20:4, 7).

WRONG PEOPLE OFTEN IMAGINE THEY ARE RIGHT

That this was the sin of the Pharisees is evident from our Lord's constant-condemnation of their self-righteousness. The ruling idea of his Sermon on the Mount was *righteousness.* The kingdom he spoke of was inwardly one of righteousness as its outstanding character. The whole of his discourse is taken up with this theme in contrast, not only with habits of living, but also with traditional maxims. As Professor Stalker states in *The Ethic of Jesus,* "Through the Sermon on the Mount, from first to last, there runs a strain of the most passionate moral earnestness. Never elsewhere in the world has there been taught so inward or difficult a morality; but it was to be the high prerogative of the Kingdom of God to realise it." Continuing his piquant contrasts, Jesus warned, "Take heed that ye do not pour righteousness before men, to be seen of them" (Matt. 6:1). True Christian righteousness is first inward. The so-called righteousness of the scribes and Pharisees was external, but that which Jesus taught was internal. The righteousness of those he exposed was made up of ostentatious words and actions; his righteousness we are to earnestly seek flows from the innermost thoughts and feelings. Those who trusted, not in God, but in themselves, had a conventional righteousness, that is, a brand intended only for the eye of society, but Christ's was a righteousness of the conscience, having regard only for God's eye.

The Pharisees were taken up with an outward show of righteousness and were the wrong people who imagined they were right, hence, the appeal of Jesus, "Except your righteousness shall exceed the righteousness of the scribes and Pharisees, ye shall in no case enter into the kingdom of heaven" (Matt. 5:20). The rest of the Sermon on the

Mount is actually an exposition of this verse, the righteousness required of Christians being contrasted first with that prescribed in the Mosaic Law and the traditional exposition of that law (Matt. 5:21–48), with contemporary Pharisaic custom (Matt. 6:1–18), and with the ordinary course of this world (Matt. 6:19 to the end of the sermon).

Repeatedly Jesus exposed the so-called *right* of the *wrong* Pharisees as having been manufactured. Their goodness was not derived from a living nature, the beauty of which is originally connected with the root from which it springs. The paraded words and deeds of the Pharisees appeared to be good, but their hearts were corrupt. They "justified themselves," were "highly esteemed among men but an abomination in the sight of God," "trusted in themselves that they were righteous, and despised others," and were not as "other men are" (Luke 10:29; 16:15; 18:9, 11, 14). The sermon of Jesus excited his avowed enemies to anger, not only because of his truly righteous life, but because he told them in no uncertain terms that righteousness must be an experience and not identified with ceremonials. If they would enter the kingdom their Pharisaism must vanish, and as sinners they must have the righteousness imputed and imparted. They must "seek his righteousness." As a teacher, Jesus demanded a height of character and attainment never even dreamed of by Moses and the prophets. He never abrogated their teachings but sharpened the edge of every precept and enlarged the scope of every principle they set forth.

THOSE WHO YEARN TO BE RIGHT CAN BE RIGHT

Jesus made it clear that the publican who could only cry, "God be merciful to me a sinner," went home *justified* rather than the Pharisee who exalted himself to such a degree as to say that he was not as low, morally, as "this publican." But yearning to be right with God, the publican found the true righteousness which the Pharisee never did because he trusted in himself that he was righteous and he despised others (Luke 18:9–14). Among the *Blesseds* of Jesus is, "Blessed are they which do hunger and thirst after righteousness; for they shall be filled [with him who is our righteousness]" (Matt. 5:6). All who yearn to be *right* before God, and are made *right,* exercise judgment of others which is right: "Judge not according to the appearance, but judge righteous judgment" (John 7:24).

Our preeminent duty, then, is to pursue that which is *right* in God's sight, even as Jesus taught, "Seek ye first the kingdom of God, and his righteousness" (Matt. 6:33). In this compelling exhortation Jesus returns to a similar one in his wonderful sermon where he instructed his own: "Lay not up for yourselves treasures on earth, where moth and rust doth corrupt, and where thieves break through and steal" (Matt. 6:19).

Those who are the Father's children must aspire to higher things—treasures in heaven—immortal pleasures of the immortal soul. They must seek, not visible wealth, but God's kingdom and

God's righteousness. What is the difference between these two eternal treasures? God's *kingdom* represents his rule, blessing, acceptance, protection, and salvation. God's *righteousness* is God's character, God's life in the soul; God the Son himself was made our righteousness, and we are to incarnate the righteousness of the kingdom.

Notice must be taken of the adjective Jesus used, *first,* meaning preceding all others. What a man endeavors to secure *first,* and chiefly, mirrors his essential character. Paul could say, "For me to live is Christ." What a man puts after "For me to live is ——," shapes his life and determines his destiny. Many perish through putting God's kingdom and his righteousness *second* in order of time. They fail to put first things *first.* Their argument is "Let us first do this or gain that, then we will seek God's kingdom." Others perish from placing the concerns of God second in order of importance. Yet if God is given the *first* place in every phase of life, then all that is necessary to life is *added,* or thrown into the bargain. If all that concerns God is our *first* concern, then all that concerns us will be his chief concern. Jesus left his own in no doubt regarding the price we must be prepared to pay if he, our righteousness, is first in all things. "Blessed are they which are persecuted for righteousness' sake: for theirs is the kingdom of heaven" (Matt. 5:10).

Seek this first—Be pure and holy
Like the Master, meek and lowly;
Yielded to His service wholly:
  Seek this first.

BOTH THE RIGHT AND THE WRONG WILL BE ULTIMATELY RECOMPENSED

Jesus spoke of a coming judgment when he will sit upon the throne of his glory to reveal who are right and who are wrong. The latter, not clothed in His righteousness, and therefore not conspicuous in righteous acts, go away into *everlasting punishment,* but the righteous in heart and action pass into *life eternal* (Matt. 25:31–46). As the Master sent the twelve forth to preach, teach, and heal, among the assurances they were cheered by was, "He that receiveth a righteous man in the name of a righteous man shall receive a righteous man's reward" (Matt. 10:41; Luke 14:14). What a day that will be when our *Jehovah Tsidkenu* returns for those made righteous by God in Christ who came the first time as the personification and perfection of righteousness!

When clothed in His brightness transported I rise,
  To meet Him in clouds of the sky,
His perfect salvation, His wonderful love,
  I'll shout with the millions on high.

BIBLE STUDY QUESTIONS

Take time to turn to each Scripture reference and mark the verse or a portion in your Bible.

1. Why is righteousness in our lives important?
2. What is the relation of righteousness to each of the Godhead?

3. Contrast God's and man's views of righteousness.
4. What is the hope of the one who wants to be right?

Appendix
A Table of Parables

It may be helpful to tabulate the outstanding parables of Jesus. Dr. A. R. Bond, in his most remarkable book, *The Master Preacher,* published way back in 1910, concluded his work with an appendix, setting forth all that Jesus said and taught. Herewith, then, with all due gratitude to the deceased author, is his valuable section on the parables. Hopefully, it will inspire the reader to further study.

THE PARABLES

I. From Early Summer 28 A.D. to Passover 29 A.D.

No.	Matthew	Mark	Luke	Name	Place
1.	13:3–9, 18–23	4:1–9, 13–20	8:5–8, 11–15	The Sower	Galilee
2.	13:24–30, 36–43			The Tares	Galilee
3.		4:26–29		The Seed Growing	Galilee
4.	13:31, 32	4:30–32		The Mustard Seed	Galilee
5.	13:33			The Leaven	Galilee
6.	13:44			The Hidden Treasure	Capernaum
7.	13:45, 46			The Goodly Pearl	Capernaum
8.	13:47–50			The Net	Capernaum

II. From Passover 29 A.D. to Autumn 29 A.D.

No.	Matthew	Mark	Luke	Name	Place
9.	18:23–35			The Unmerciful Servant	Capernaum

III. From Autumn 29 A.D. to Spring 30 A.D.

No.	Matthew	Mark	Luke	Name	Place
10.			10:25–37	The Good Samaritan	Judea
11.			11:5–13	The Midnight Friend	Judea
12.			12:16–21	The Rich Fool	Judea
13.			12:35–40	The Watchful Servants	Judea
14.			13:6–9	The Barren Fig Tree	Judea
(4)			13:18, 19	The Mustard Seed	Judea
(5)	13:33		13:20, 21	The Leaven	Judea
15.			14:7–11	The Chief Seats	Perea
16.			14:16–24	The Great Supper	Perea

17.			14:25–30	The Rash Builder	Perea
18.			14:31–35	The Rash King	Perea
19.			15:3–7	The Lost Sheep	Perea
20.			15:8–10	The Lost Coin	Perea
21.			15:11–32	The Lost Son	Perea
22.			16:1–13	The Unrighteous Steward	Perea
23.			16:19–31	The Rich Man and Lazarus	Perea
24.			17:7–10	The Unprofitable Servants	Perea
25.			18:1–8	The Unrighteous Judge	Samaria or Galilee
26.			18:9–14	The Pharisee and the Publican	Samaria or Galilee
27.	20:1–16			The Laborers in the Vineyard	Perea
28.			19:11–27	The Pounds	Jericho

IV. During Passover 30 A.D.

29.	21:28–32			The Two Sons	Jerusalem
30.	21:33–44	12:1–11	20:9–18	The Wicked Husbandman	Jerusalem
31.	22:1–13			The Royal Marriage	Jerusalem
32.	24:32, 33	13:28, 29	21:29–31	The Fig Tree Leaving	Mt. Olivet
33.	25:1–13			The Ten Virgins	Mt. Olivet
34.	25:14–30			The Ten Talents	Mt. Olivet

Bibliography

Barnes, Albert. *Barnes' Notes on the New Testament.* Grand Rapids: Kregel Publications, n.d.

Bernard, T. D. *The Central Teaching of Jesus Christ.* London: Oxford Press, 1920.

Bond, A. R. *The Master Preacher.* New York: American Tract Society, 1910.

Dale, R. W. *Christian Doctrine.* London: Hodder & Stoughton, n.d.

DeFoe, James. *Guide to Bible Study.* London: Society of Christian Knowledge, 1908.

———. *History of the Bible.* London: Gety, 1853.

Ellicott, Charles H. *Commentary on the Whole Bible.* Grand Rapids: Zondervan, 1951.

Fairbairn, A. M. *Studies in the Life of Christ.* London: Hodder & Stoughton, 1900. A spiritual treasure all Bible students should have.

Glover, Richard. *The Gospel of Matthew.* Grand Rapids: Zondervan, 1956.

———. *History of Jesus.* Grand Rapids: Zondervan, 1956.

Glover, T. R. *The Jesus of History.* London: Student Christian Movement, 1917.

Godet, F. *Godet's Commentary on the New Testament.* New York: Funk & Wagnalls, 1886.

Gore, Charles. *Jesus of Nazareth.* London: Thornton Butterworth Ltd., 1917.

Green, Peter. *Our Lord and Saviour.* London: Longmans, Green & Co., 1928.

Halley, Henry H. *Halley's Bible Handbook.* Grand Rapids: Zondervan, 1927.

Handbook of Christian Teaching. London: Sheldon Press, 1939.

Hastings, James. *Dictionary of the Bible.* Edinburgh: T. & T. Clark, 1909.

Hodgkin, Henry T. *Jesus among Men.* London: Student Christian Movement, 1930.

The International Standard Bible Encyclopedia. Grand Rapids: Wm. Erdmans, 1929. See articles on topics with which we have dealt.

Lange, John Peter. *Commentary on the Holy Scriptures.* New York: Scribner's, 1884.

Lee, Umphrey. *The Life of Christ.* Nashville: Cokesbury Press, 1926.

Liddon. H. B. *The Divinity of Our Lord.* London: Pickering & Inglis, 1864.

Lockyer, Herbert. *All the Children of the Bible.* Grand Rapids: Zondervan, 1970.

———. *All the Miracles of the Bible.* Grand Rapids: Zondervan, 1961.

———. *All the Parables of the Bible.* Grand Rapids: Zondervan, 1963.

Macartney, Clarence E. *What Jesus Really Taught.* Nashville: Abingdon Press, 1958.

Mackintosh, H. R. *The Doctrine of the Person of Christ.* International Theological Library. New York: Scribner's, 1912.

Moorehead, W. E. *Old and New Testament Outline Studies.* New York: Revell, 1893.

Morgan, G. Campbell. *The Teaching of Christ.* London: Marshall, Morgan, & Scott, 1930.

Patterson, W. P. *Christ and the Gospels.* Edinburgh: T. & T. Clark, 1911.

Pierson, A. T. *Knowing the Scriptures.* London: James Nisbet Co., 1910.

Scroggie, W. Graham. *A Guide to the Gospels.* London: Pickering & Inglis, 1948.

Stalker, James. *The Christology of Jesus.* London: Hodder & Stoughton, 1899.

———. *The Ethic of Jesus.* London: Hodder & Stoughton, 1919.

Vincent, Marvin R. *Word Studies in the New Testament.* New York: Scribner's, 1882.

Warfield, Benjamin B. *The Lord of Glory.* London: Hodder & Stoughton, 1909.

Wescott, B. F. *The Gospels.* Edinburgh: T. & T. Clark, 1884.

Whyte, Alexander. *The Walk, Conversation, and Character of Jesus Christ Our Lord.* London: Oliphant, n.d.